King Sugar

King Sugar

Jamaica, the Caribbean and the World Sugar Economy

Michelle Harrison

© 2001 Michelle Harrison   All rights reserved
First published in 2001 by Latin America Bureau
(Research and Action) Ltd,
1 Amwell Street, London EC1R 1UL

The Latin America Bureau is an independent research and publishing organisation. It works to broaden public understanding of issues of human rights and social and economic justice in Latin America and the Caribbean.

A CIP catalogue record for this book is available from the British Library
ISBN: 1 899365 38 9

First published in the USA by New York University Press

Editing: Jean McNeil
Cover painting: Gaston Tabois
Cover design: Andy Dark
Design: Liz Morrell

Printed by Russell Press, Nottingham

Dedicated to the memory of my dear friend Alison

Acknowledgements

There is a long list of people to whom I am greatly indebted. Here I can thank just a few, and hope that the many others realise that the gratitude I expressed to them in person was heartfelt.

First of all, thanks to all of my hosts in Trelawny, whose enormous hospitality will never be forgotten. I am indebted to the hundreds of families who were willing to share their stories with me, and to one in particular who provided me with a home – and an alternative perspective – during my long periods of fieldwork. In addition, it is fair to say that without Leonie Campbell and her family, the research and writing of this book could never have happened.

Professor Don Robotham, previously at UWI (Mona Campus), provided wonderful support and insight during fieldwork. Dr. Ian Cook (University of Birmingham, UK), who shared fieldwork triumphs and tragedies, has been a tremendous source of intellectual stimulation over the last decade. Undoubtedly, he is the original source of some of the ideas presented in this book. Closer to home, Gordon and Maureen Harrison provided me with a quiet place to write some of the earlier chapters of the book, and Gordon was a brilliant first draft copy editor. Thanks too to Christine Bull, who was an enthusiastic guest researcher.

I am grateful to all at the Latin America Bureau, particularly Jim Ferguson and Jean McNeil, for their support, skill, and patience beyond the call of duty. Thanks also to Tony Hannah, Head of Economics and Statistics at the International Sugar Office in London for his help on sourcing statistics.

The deepest debt, however, is owed to my husband, Nick Bull, who made many sacrifices in order to see this book completed.

Contents

Introduction

From Caribbean sugarmill
to global supermarket

The sugar-cane industry is not a fashionable one in the Caribbean. Over recent decades many of the islands of the region have fought hard to diversify and now boast high-value extractive industries, exclusive tourism resorts and manufacturing sectors. The people of the Caribbean work and travel globally, and their cultural capital is a world export. From this perspective the sugar industry is viewed as archaic – a remnant of a colonial past and an abhorrent social history that remains synonymous with poverty and struggle. Yet the imprint that the common history of cane cultivation has left on the landscape of the region is indelible. Even as the importance of the modern day industry fades, it continues in many important ways to shape the present circumstances of national economies as well as peoples' lives.

Since its first cultivation in the Caribbean, sugar has shaped much more than the region's own economy and identity. In recent history Caribbean sugar has become intertwined with post-war development agendas, the geopolitics of the Cold War, and the era of structural adjustment; in the distant past, the profits of the plantations fuelled the industrial revolution in Britain. The same revenue flows that once propelled the infamous 'triangular trade' today contribute to global corporatism, while the system of insurance developed in the City of London to back the transatlantic voyages of old has evolved into the 'futures' markets of present. Indeed, the history of the Caribbean sugar industry provides us with a window on many of the important features of the development of the modern world economy, and the linkages between North and South, wealth and poverty, producer and consumer – in contemporary times, the Caribbean cane cutter and global supermarket shopper.

The sugar trade may have propelled growth on a global scale, but it has given little back to the islands. Their national economies are skewed and indebted, and the physical beauty of their rural landscapes is in sharp

1

contrast to the socio-economic desperation common in the sugar growing areas. Despite diversification, sugar is still a significant earner of foreign exchange for several of the Caribbean islands, and an important source of employment. In Jamaica, for example, it provides the third most important source of revenue and, critically, is still the single largest employer of labour on the island. Yet at the local and the national level the industry faces acute problems related to an historic lack of investment, poor pay and inadequate field and factory practices. Protected for decades from the vagaries of the world market by special trade arrangements with Britain and the European Union, the industry currently fails to operate at a level that is anywhere near efficient on the world stage. This presents the region with a serious development dilemma.

The Caribbean sugar industry is not just inefficient – with the exception of Cuba, it has also become inconsequential on a global level. As a result, over the first few years of the next decade it faces a crisis unparalleled in its history. A series of inter-related international policy developments threaten, at the very least, to reduce the value of the preferential agreements upon which the sugar islands depend; at worst, any form of 'special relationship' characterised by favourable trading terms with customer countries will be cancelled. These developments bode the final curtain call for an industry that has always lurched from crisis to crisis. But this time, the structures and relationships that have saved it in the past are no longer in place.

As the Caribbean faces an historical turning point, this book attempts to bring together many of the disparate threads of the region's sugar story. It begins and ends in the Jamaican village of Gaythorne[1], with the people who live each day within the confines of a local plantation economy. In between, it maps the contemporary international forces and historical events that have helped to shape local circumstance. Using first hand accounts it examines each part of the production and consumption chain – the dealer on the futures market, the multinational executive, the Caribbean industry expert. In so doing it explores the machinations of the global commodity markets, the nature of the institutions of international governance and the positioning of the Caribbean in the international economic order. Most importantly, it considers the region's struggles with the industry over recent times, considers its role in the

---

[1] Gaythorne is a pseudonym used to protect the identity of the author's informants and the village that formed the focus of her study.

modern Caribbean, and poses the questions: what are the prospects for the pockets of plantation economy that have remained trapped by their history? What will a post-sugar future look like?

Chapter one opens with a local level account of the circumstances of production of cane sugar in the Jamaican village of Gaythorne, where the landscape of cane fields and plantation houses tells the history of three hundred years of colonialism. Through the voices of the people of Gaythorne and the local managers of the sugar industry, the day-to-day realities of poverty, struggle and resistance are explored. So too are the local nuances of the crisis in the industry. Sugar is the root that feeds the branches of the local economy of Gaythorne, yet it exists in self-perpetuating economic jeopardy. Land inequality, the stagnation of domestic agriculture and the lack of diversification of the local economy all contribute to the conundrum. The people of Gaythorne explain for themselves the dilemma they are faced with: the sugar industry is generally loathed and associated with appalling working conditions and wholly inadequate pay, yet its decline means unprecedented hardship.

Chapter two is concerned with sugar as a commodity. It explains the relationship between the sugar producing islands of the Caribbean and international trade and that between the poverty of the cane cutters of Gaythorne and the problems associated with the commodity markets. Within an environment of international rivalry and protectionism, the international trade of sugar has been conditioned by unstable market characteristics and oversupply since the early colonial period. The sugar-cane producers of the Caribbean and other less developed regions of the world are still living with the legacy of historical inequalities in the trading system, as they face continuing 'unfair' competition from beet sugar grown in the North. The chapter explores the vagaries of the 'world market', the role of the institutions of global governance and special trade arrangements. It also considers the trade trap that means that the Caribbean sugar producers have little choice but to carry on growing sugar to sell internationally even though it does not appear in their best interests to do so. Sugar as a commodity has tied the Caribbean into a contradictory and negative set of rules, the same ones which now condition the international aspect of the crisis.

Sugar as big business is the focus of chapter three, with a contemporary analysis of the relationship between corporate interests, world trade and sugar production in the Caribbean. From the point of view of individuals on the Futures trading desks and those involved in the sugar industry in Jamaica, and in terms of the commodity trade described in chapter two, the links are drawn along the chain from production to consumption. The effects of transnational corporations on the economies of the South are extraordinarily difficult to measure, and in no other area of development is there a bigger gap between governmental and NGO thinking than over the value or otherwise of global corporations. This chapter explores the arguments from the North as well as the South, and looks at the recent history and contemporary nature of corporate involvement in Jamaica. In addition, it outlines the position of corporatism in relation to the current international policy conundrum.

The historical account of the relationship between sugar, the Caribbean and Britain in chapter four places the current crisis in context. The development of the 'sweet tooth' for which the British are renowned was entirely dependent upon the establishment of sugar production in the islands of the Caribbean, and the chapter explores how, in both an economic and social sense, the history of the sugar islands has been intimately connected with that of European development. Over the course of three centuries the discussion takes in the development of mercantilism and capitalism, and the relationship between global political economy and the plantations of Jamaica and the other islands. It considers how, within the islands, sugar was a total institution that completely conditioned the developing social and economic structure. Moreover, it considers too the beginning of the relationship between American foreign policy and business interests in relation to sugar, which have had profound effects on the region in the twentieth century.

Following on from this historical narrative, chapter five looks at the struggles of the sugar islands in the twentieth century to overcome the brutal associations of the sugar industry and poverty. The post war period has been concerned with alleviating the economic dependence on the sugar industry, but it has also been clouded by the politics of the Cold War and the spectre of debt, which have influenced both the path of development and the role of the cane cultivation. In the latter half of the century, different economic philosophies have been variously applied to the islands of the Caribbean, and in various ways, monoculture has been overcome. But the timeless conflict between plantation and domestic agriculture lingers and economic dependence upon sugar remains. The chapter profiles Jamaica, Barbados, Cuba and the Dominican Republic, each of which face a 'personalised' crisis in the face of international circumstances. By understanding the idiosyncrasies of their struggles over the twentieth century we can gain a clearer perspective of the possibilities for the 'post sugar' era.

Chapter six concludes with a short perspective on the future of the region. Back in Gaythorne, the young and the elderly discuss their views on development possibilities outside of the sugar model. This is juxtaposed with a realistic appraisal of the constraints faced by these debt-burdened small island economies. For several hundred years sugar has linked the Caribbean with Europe. Some thought needs to be given to alternative ways to preserve this link into the future – this time with thought to a more enlightened consumer and equitable chain from producer to supermarket shelf.

Chapter One

Living with the Sugar Legacy: Life on a Jamaican Plantation

'Them just work you hard for little money. Them work you hard, and you have nothing to show for it but tough hands.' (woman cane field worker, aged 55)

At the height of the sugar-cane harvesting season in the late spring in the Jamaican village of Gaythorne, small field gangs of cane cutters labour hard with machetes under the sun. As men chop down the ten-foot stalks in the dense green foliage, women tie the canes into bundles for transportation to the nearby Long Pond sugar factory, where grinders and boilers extract a sticky mass of molasses and unrefined sugar. In this plantation community few households escape the arduous demands of the cane-harvesting season. The sugar industry is the backbone of the local economy and most people in Gaythorne either work in it or are supported by someone who does.

The physical setting for these harsh labours, however, is spectacular. From the vantage point of the escarpments that rise on either side of the narrow valley along which Gaythorne spreads, there is a panoramic view across the ragged limestone hills of Trelawny parish. Below, the steep slopes on both sides of Gaythorne valley are thickly wooded; along the valley floor the community appears as a thin squiggle, half a mile long, lining the main road as it winds its way back out into open country. To the east and west on the valley bottom, as far as the eye can see and covering every apparent stretch of available land, are the endless fields of sugar cane; a light green blanket against the fern green of the hillsides. From this vantage point it seems a perfect scene of Jamaican rural charm.

But walk along the path down the hillside and you will encounter signs of the legacy of the sugar industry: the dilapidated single-roomed wooden huts that are family homes; the communal tap; the pit latrine; the old men carrying machetes as they climb past on their long journey to farm their small 'squatted' plots of land far up on the hillsides.

Leave Gaythorne and travel east a few miles through the sugar cane to the village of Clarks Town, where the noise of the machinery in the Long Pond sugar factory provides a constant background hum. Long Pond is an enduring feature of Trelawny's eighteenth-century role as the thriving centre of the island's sugar industry and one of the two estates in the parish that result from the amalgamations of the original eighty-nine that were in operation during the slavery period. The closures and amalgamations that have led to this concentration over time are marked by the old Great Houses and stone mills that dot the 19,000 acres of Long Pond land. These lasting features on the physical landscape are symbols of the hold of the sugar industry on the scattered communities. In these plantation pockets of Jamaica, time really does seem to have stood still.

It has not, of course. Time has moved on, but the grip of poverty remains. Real economic development has been thwarted by the legacy of cane – by its domination of farmland, capital resources and labour. There are young people in Gaythorne whose entrepreneurial spirit is thwarted by destitution; there are elderly people who, during their lives, have had to travel across the world to find other work. Time has moved on and so have the ideals and aspirations of Gaythorne people, but the industry, by virtue of lack of alternative, has managed to maintain its grasp on the community. In this chapter we meet some of those people who struggle daily with the dilemmas of the plantation economy, and consider the role of an arcane industry in modern Jamaica.

Rural life

There are about 460 households in Gaythorne: of these, about 300 are dependent upon the sugar industry. Life for rural Jamaicans, who constitute more than half of the island's population, is generally harder than that of their urban compatriots, but those who depend upon the sugar industry suffer even more than most. People in the community live in homes made from concrete or wood; those working in the cane fields are most likely to live in the smallest or most dilapidated houses. Only 60% of households have electricity and just 40% have a water tap in their yard; for those who depend primarily on the sugar industry for their survival, this falls to less

Cutting cane, Azua, Dominican Republic   *Sean Sprague/Panos Pictures*

than a half, and less than a third, respectively. Very few own modern conveniences: less than half of the community has a fridge or a television, and some homes do not even have a radio. 'Sugar' households, moreover, are in general less likely than their neighbours to own consumer goods. And in a community where education is held in high regard for the economic and social mobility that it can generate, it is common for the children of sugar workers to be unable to attend school continuously because their families are unable to provide them with food for their lunch, or money for their books.

The basis of the poverty of rural Jamaicans resides not just in the pitiful wages paid by the sugar industry, but in the inequality of land distribution and the stagnation of domestic agriculture, that the cane plantations have generated. Historically, the sugar industry has dominated both the best agricultural land on the island and the resources afforded to agriculture as a whole. In common with many poor nations, the agricultural sector in Jamaica forms the basis of the rural economy: according to official statistics it remains the single largest employer of labour in the country, engaging around a quarter of the labour force. But agriculture in the island, and across the Caribbean as a whole, has always been riven by the conflict

9

between the plantation sector producing for export and the so-called 'small-farm' sector that produces some export crops but farms primarily for domestic consumption.

Within the confines of plantation agriculture independent farmers – as they came to be known after emancipation – were forced onto the steep hillsides or most marginal strips of land around the edges of the sugar cane fields. This pattern has persisted until today: the island's latest agricultural census indicates that 82% of farmers have less than five acres each, and hold in total 16% of the island's farmland. Conversely, less than 1% of farmers have more than a hundred acres each, and between them control 57% of land.

Nowhere in rural Jamaica is this conflict between the small-farm cultivator and the plantation enterprise more obvious than in the remaining sugar cane areas, and in villages like Gaythorne. Most households in Gaythorne, for instance, farm food crops, but few have access to what they consider to be adequate land. Most have less than five acres to farm; only a handful have more than ten. Moreover, the majority of this land is rented, or squatted, from the Long Pond sugar estate. Gaythorne farmers often have to travel several miles through the sugar cane by foot or by donkey even to reach their 'ground', where they attempt to grow food for their families. On the thin and stony soil that they have access to, most also grow cane as well as an essential source of income, and thus have even less land, time and energy for their food crops. Jamaica is indeed a green and lush island, but the reality is that very few of its independent farmers are able to make even a reasonable living. Recent studies have even suggested that as many as ten per cent of rural children suffer from malnutrition.

Unsurprisingly, these deeply embedded structures of underdevelopment meant that the agricultural sector failed to benefit from the general economic growth that the island experienced in the post-Second World War period. As bauxite mining, tourism and manufacturing emerged to become Jamaica's principal foreign exchange earners, relative agricultural productivity actually declined. Despite investment in the sector, production of sugar and other commercial crops has continued to fall; moreover, as domestic production has fallen further, more and more of the food that Jamaicans eat has to be imported. At the national level this has had disastrous consequences for the macro economy, but at the local level it has meant the greater entrenchment of rural poverty.

In Gaythorne, as agricultural wages have failed to grow in line with the economy as a whole, many try to avoid working in agriculture altogether and instead seek work in bauxite mining, in a factory or in a hotel. But generally these industries are small 'enclaves' which employ relatively few people. The rural economy is not sufficiently diversified to allow people to escape from land-based work. Outside of the poorly paid seasonal work that the sugar estate offers, regular waged employment is rare. The norm, then, as we will see in the discussion below, is *occupational multiplicity* – many people mix their work in the sugar industry and their domestic farming with whatever irregular work they may be able to get outside of the agricultural sector. The survival strategies of most of the households in Gaythorne are thus a brave and tenacious mix of seasonal, irregular and part-time sources of support.

Not only do rural Jamaicans suffer both absolutely and relatively from poverty, and from under- and unemployment, but they also lack essential services and infrastructure such as medical care and public utilities like electricity and water. The island's urban areas are better serviced, and also offer a greater chance of regular waged employment. It is therefore no surprise that outmigration from rural Jamaica is a social institution. Migration is, in fact, an institutionalised aspect of Caribbean societies as a whole. Although it is the movement to the UK, US and Canada since 1950 that has attracted most attention over the last 30 years, rural-urban migration has actually been the dominant demographic trend.

Since the 1950s, rural growth rates have stalled at below 1% – lower than the overall population growth rate – as migrants have left the rural areas for the island's capital and tourist towns. Because young men and women are more likely than others to migrate to urban areas in search of employment, this movement has resulted in higher concentrations of children and older people in the areas of population loss. In Gaythorne – as in so many other rural communities – grandparents and other relations take care of the children who remain within the security of the community as their parents migrate temporarily, or even permanently, in search of work. But the strength of the ties are such that the remittances received from the migrants are the community's most essential source of economic support.

Life for most of those in Gaythorne, then, is clearly no idyll. It is tough and unpredictable, and filled with all of the social and physical insecurities that are associated with grinding poverty. Those living in the shadow of the sugar industry have long witnessed the injustice of their circumstances. Not only are they just a few miles from the luxury tourist hotels that grace the island's north coast, but most importantly they are a community that, through their own migrations and those of their kin, have global relationships and awareness. And in recent years, as an increasing trickle of migrants have returned home to retire after two or three decades abroad, so this awareness has increased as the socio-economic divisions within their own community have become more apparent.

Savings from years of work in England or the United States, or an English pension, mean that returning migrants can replace the small wooden houses on their plots with imposing brick homes. They can invest in small businesses to supplement their pensions and save their money in foreign exchange accounts to protect themselves from the devaluation of the Jamaican dollar. Or they can buy a sizeable piece of land for cane and pay others to work in it for them. All in all, the majority of Gaythorne people are aware of the development dilemmas of their own community, and the role of the sugar industry within it.

It is this awareness that contributes to many of the contradictions that have classically beset rural Jamaica: the high attachment to land, yet the low esteem commonly afforded to agricultural work; the long-standing complaints about the shortage of labour in the sugar industry in what is known to be a labour surplus economy; and the dichotomy between the hatred of work in the cane fields and the riots that in the past have prevented the introduction of labour-saving mechanical harvesters. What is the role of the sugar industry in modern Jamaica? What does the industry's crisis mean for rural people's livelihoods? What other types of opportunities might there be to take its place? The voices of those from Gaythorne will help us begin to understand these issues.

Gaythorne and Long Pond: enduring an unhappy marriage

The grasp of the sugar industry upon Gaythorne and the other rural communities across the parish of Trelawny has been strong and long-standing. Trelawny as a whole was established in 1771 at the height of the island's sugar prosperity and it quickly became the thriving centre of its sugar economy. However, with more plantations than any other parish in the island, Trelawny also became the centre of resistance to the industry – with the Trelawny Maroons and the 1831 slave rebellion in Jamaica's western parishes standing out as landmarks in the history of Caribbean slave resistance.

Falmouth, the parish capital, was the seat of the famous William Knibb's Ministry – the nonconformist Baptist Minister who led the fight against slavery. It was the same nonconformists who, after emancipation, went on to lead the Free Village Movement, fighting to acquire land from the hands of the plantocracy (planters or landed wealthy) on which communities for newly freed Jamaicans could be established. Although the history of Gaythorne has not been clearly documented, it is likely that it was established around this time and within the jurisdiction of this movement. From the beginning the local sugar estate provided one of the few post-emancipation sources of employment. Deprived of land and with virtually no alternative work available, Jamaicans were practically indentured to the sugar plantation.

Records of Long Pond date from 1753, when a sugar factory and rum distillery began operation. Crop records of 1780 indicate a production of 165 hogsheads of sugar and 85 puncheons of rum, which was an output typical of the other small plantations existing in the parish at the time. The history of the estate during the eighteenth and nineteenth centuries is not well documented but it would appear that during the rationalisation (explored in chapter four) of the sugar industry of the nineteenth century Long Pond factory survived as a central unit – and, as the collapse of the industry led to the abandonment or sale of surrounding estates, amalgamation greatly increased its acreage. During this period the smaller family concerns were probably bought out by large investors.

In the early years of the present century, Long Pond estate was owned by Sheriff and Co Ltd, a Scottish concern based in Glasgow – this pattern of foreign ownership being typical of the Caribbean sugar industry as a whole at this time. In 1953 it was acquired by and became a wholly owned subsidiary of Seagrams Ltd of Canada, the huge distilling company. In the 1970s Long Pond was nationalised and remained under the control of the National Sugar Company Ltd until 1994, when it fell once again into private hands. Latterly, however, this has involved a consortium of Jamaican interests rather than the classic foreign ownership of yesteryear.

It is likely that Long Pond – or the smaller sugar estates that have since been amalgamated into Long Pond – has owned much of the land surrounding Gaythorne since the community was first established; today, it dominates the landscape to the largest extent. Long Pond Sugar Company

The Long Pond estate in Trelawny, a few miles inland from the hotels.   *Michelle Harrison*

is comprised of a sugar factory and approximately 19,000 acres of land. Of this, only 4,700 acres are actually under cane. More than half the total acreage is marginal hillside and forestry not suitable for cane and is officially unused (some, unofficially, is 'squatted' on by Gaythorne farmers). Long Pond grows canes itself on about 3,500 acres of its land. A further 1,000, through a long established relationship, is leased to local farmers – many from Gaythorne – who grow canes to sell back to Long Pond. The factory processes canes from its own lands together with those from another 2,500 acres of privately cultivated small-farmer lands. This involves more than 2,000 people in all, some living miles away from Gaythorne, who have to haul their canes considerable distances to deliver them to the factory.

In addition to the market it provides for the canes grown by these farmers, Long Pond provides work directly for more than a thousand people over the course of a year. As we will see below, the type of work available varies between the most low status employment (for more than half of the total of employees) in 'the field'; to the slightly better paid jobs in the factory for about 400; and the revered administrative positions for just a handful of middle-class Jamaicans. But this work is seasonal; indeed, Gaythorne has had to respond to the rhythms of the sugar industry throughout its history.

During the 'crop', when the canes are cut – usually between January and July – work is frenetic. The canes have to be cut and harvested, and transported across fields and pot-holed roads to reach the factory. For the months of the crop, the factory is expected to operate continually through the day and night in order for the canes to be processed. For the rest of the year – the 'dead' season – work in the field continues as the canes are replanted and the soil weeded and fertilised. The factory too, remains open for maintenance work. But those who are poor during the 'crop' are likely to be even poorer in the leaner months. On a wider scale, the momentum of the sugar industry drives the local economy; out-of-crop, the effects of deepened poverty are felt in the small grocery shops, the workshops of the self-employed tradesperson, and in the rum bars. During the crop, local tailors are busier making new clothes, school books are bought, and new livestock purchased. In this way, sugar cane dominates not just the landscape, but the livelihoods of all who live within its hinterland. It is the root that feeds the branches of the local economy.

A window on the sugar industry's problems

'The economic situation is so bad that absenteeism is getting worse... the workers are getting paid so little, so they're not turning up... This is getting much worse – they don't think that working makes much sense. They won't work Saturday because the money goes in taxes – they don't see anything for their money.'

(Male factory foreman, 40 years old)

The crisis in the sugar industry has global dimensions, but in Trelawny at the local level the financial, technological and, critically, the social constraints on its operations are obvious. Work in the sugar factory is hampered by aged machinery and years of disinvestment. Similarly, cane yields from estate lands are curbed by poor field management practices. Perhaps most daunting, however, is the issue of labour relations. Workers generally loathe the management, while the management complain of the antipathy of their employees. Despite the desperate shortage of alternative employment, labour shortages are common in the fields. The socio-cultural history of the sugar industry has left an indelible imprint that is only reinforced by the appalling working conditions that the industry still offers today.

Sugar cane has been grown in Jamaica for over three hundred years. It's an agricultural product that survives the ravages of drought and hurricane, and, in terms of its husbandry, is relatively low maintenance. Yet, across the island of Jamaica, the industry fails to operate at a level of efficiency that is anywhere near competitive on the world stage. The historical 'rot' set into the island's industry as far back as the nineteenth century; more recently, the policy conundrum of international trade has supported highly inefficient levels of productivity.

Long Pond has been one of the island's worst cases over the last ten years. It only produces around 14,000 tonnes of sugar each year, which on occasion has collapsed to just 8,000. And its TC:TS ratios (the tons of cane needed to produce a single ton of sugar) have been amongst the highest on the island. 'Downtime' – the percentage of time during the 'crop' when the factory is not in operation because of breakdowns, has been as high as 44% at Long Pond during 1998. This is easy to understand given that a new sugar factory has not been built in Jamaica since the 1940s. The inefficiencies of 'downtime' are huge: not only because they interrupt the supposed 24 hour regime of sugar production during 'crop', but also because of their impact upon the workforce. As the Chairman of Long Pond described it:

> 'it can get to the stage that if the factory stayed running for a week, half the workforce would drop down dead with shock.'

Although cane is not a difficult crop to grow, the yield of cane produced per acre and the yield of sugar produced per ton of cane will vary widely according to farming techniques. Even according to Jamaican standards, Long Pond has been producing extremely low yields on both scores. Not only have field practices generally been inadequate, in terms of the use of cane varieties and the regularity of replanting, but the cultivation of the cane is severely hampered by transport and infrastructure problems. The procedure of cutting the cane, piling it up into trucks and transporting it to the factory can present Long Pond with serious problems. Cane must be milled when it is fresh, as its sugar content declines rapidly after cutting as the sucrose is eaten away by bacteria. Indeed, after three days cane is usually too 'stale' to be worth milling.

Cane is one of the bulkiest crops that can be grown, but often after it is cut the trucks fail to arrive in the field or the 'grab' (the mechanical loader) breaks down and the canes have to be laboriously piled up by

A tractor pulls a barge of sugar cane to the mill, Guyana   *Duncan Simpson/Panos Pictures*

hand. Many cane fields are in remote or inaccessible locations; the pot-holed lanes that lead to them can become unnavigable in poor weather. Some cane never even reaches the factory but may even rot in the fields and much of that which does arrive is already beginning to go stale.

If the problems that are experienced on the estate cane lands are serious, then those suffered by the independent small cane farmers are even worse. Indeed, the organisation of the harvesting and transport of the thousands of small farmers who sell their canes to the estate presents a logistical nightmare, and it is small wonder that any of it arrives at the factory on time.

Those in senior management positions in the sugar industry point to other domestic issues that they believe have constrained its development over the last two decades. These relate to the *realpolitik* of sugar on the island: the way in which its price has allegedly been suppressed to subsidise other industries and keep foodstuffs cheap; the inertia of government and its failure to push forward the implementation of new developments in plant husbandry; and its absolute refusal from the 1960s onwards to allow the large-scale mechanisation of the cane harvesting operation.

17

The huge dependence upon the labour-intensive nature of cane has contributed to the general inertia. In the post-war period the development emphasis has been on diversification away from the sugar economy rather than development within it, as the importance of tourism has increased and business and service sectors have emerged in the urban economy. The sugar industry has suffered not just from macro-economic constraints, but from a lack of capital investment, and an inability to attract the island's brightest and best young people.

During the 'crop' it is common for the industry to experience at least two island-wide strikes and pay disputes. The 'bad blood' between the management and workforce is inherited from the industry's distant history, and from the post-colonial period when each estate continued to exploit their workforce to the limit. At Long Pond these disputes have often flared up into scenes of outright hostility and physical threats. In 1991 the then-manager of the estate was forced to abandon his position after a strike by field and factory workers who, citing management corruption as the cause for Long Pond's economic malaise, refused to 'start the crop' unless new management was installed. The general manager and three other members of his senior staff were dismissed, narrowly escaping the crowds of angry workers gathered around the Long Pond offices. More recently, during the 1998 crop at Long Pond, four full weeks of production were lost to strike action over pay and conditions.

It is probably fair to acknowledge that in recent years, and under a new estate manager at Long Pond, there has been a growing awareness of the plight of the workers. In fact this recognition is island-wide, and those in positions of national authority readily accept that the current terms and conditions of unemployment are economically and socially unsustainable. Pay has increased slightly: in the early 1990s the average worker at Long Pond was receiving a little over the equivalent of one pound sterling a day but in recent years there have been two pay increases. The average salary for a full-time field worker in the industry is now around £30 per week (bearing in mind the average cost of goods in a Jamaican supermarket would be more expensive than those in England). But at the same time as labour costs have risen, the industry has had to cope with two reductions in the price of sugar. As the current Long Pond manager explains:

'the situation is very grim to say the least. Levels of production have not increased to equate with rising labour costs, and I can't get the money to invest in the factory. It is very difficult to explain the bottom line to the workers, and even more difficult to get them to believe you.'

Indeed, such is the crisis within the Jamaican sugar industry that even those in management positions allude to the invisible chains that constrain them. At the local level there are serious problems with labour relations, poor infrastructure, a shortage of capital and inadequate machinery; at the national level these problems are compounded (as chapter two explains) by structural adjustment. Below, the owner of a sugar estate in Jamaica explains at length in his own words the dilemmas that the industry faces:

'In my view, the biggest problem is the mentality of the sugar industry – that it's not really a business but a way of life. And the factories that are remaining require major expenditure – they are small by international standards... we've been through a period where sugar has not really made money and therefore there is no money to reinvest from the industry. Getting money from outside is not really an option, because the returns at the moment are not sufficient for someone to go and borrow from the bank. The interest rates are 70%.

Another of the problems which underlies everything is the level of technical skills that people employed in the industry have, both in the factory and on the agricultural side. Farmers and those people who work on the estate... A lot of people cannot read and write – and it is very difficult to train people and increase their knowledge efficiently and quickly when they can't read – also they can't read instructions on how to use herbicides. And they have to use things that are poisonous and dangerous....

Because the skills are low, we are not mechanised to the extent that other sugar industries around the world are. And that goes from the person who works on the boilers in the factories to the person who drives a tractor. There is a lot of resistance to change because people actually require the skill over years and years. Sugar does not attract the best calibre of people. We can't pay sufficient money in order to get enough people in the industry in order to raise its productivity. Also we have a problem because most of the factories are out in the middle of the bush and qualified people don't want to be an electrical engineer out in the middle of the bush.

There are many reasons for the lack of mechanisation. Some in the past have been political and social. If we are to compete sufficiently and reduce our costs, in order to make sufficient money to reinvest and to improve the whole operation, both the growing and the manufacturing of sugar, then we are going to have to mechanise.

And small farmers will increasingly have to be left out. To be anywhere near efficient you need to be growing at least 500 acres of cane; some of our cane farmers are growing less than an acre. In the future, the estates need to grow as much of the cane as they can, together with being supplied by very large independent farmers who have at least 500 acres. And that land must be producing at least 25 tonnes of cane per acre. Anything less is not viable, but we've got small farmers producing 10 or 12 tonnes on their acre. They just can't afford the fertiliser, the labour, the outlay necessary.

If we don't take the money from our industry now, and use it to improve our efficiency, come 2010, or whenever it is, there isn't going to be this safety net. And the factories that cannot produce, or cannot make a profit as part of a company, are going to go to the wall. And I'm sure of that. There is no way that we can survive in the very long term on world market prices.

The fact is that no one wants to work in sugar because its menial and people don't get paid enough, but at the same time no one wants to pay anything more for their pound of sugar. There are not enough people who are coming into the industry who are willing to get their hands dirty. I wouldn't want to go out and cut cane. I wouldn't want to go out and spread fertiliser by hand. I wouldn't want to go out and pick out weeds out of the fields. But we provide a source of employment, although at the same time we are still stuck with this slavery stigma. And a woman spreading fertiliser by hand in the field when a tractor and fertiliser spreader can do it much more efficiently – or rather much more quickly and timely – is morally wrong but socially required. Because what is that woman going to do? If she is the only breadwinner? If she has to look after her invalid husband and she is 55, what do we do?

Table 1
Normal annual production in tonnes

Barbados	70,000
Jamaica	2,300,00
St Kitts	25,000
Trinidad & Tobago	120,000

Source: ACP Group aide-memoire on ACP sugar, January 2000

The industry does not have the money to pay a pension that is anywhere decent. People have to work until they die. Now if we mechanise we would have less people; we would be able to pay them more and still save money. The industry could save money. We would have fewer people to train to a correct standard so we'd be able to spend the money to do it. We could end up with a partially automated operation. That would work for the estates because they hold the better land. How the farmers are going to tackle that – well, that's another thing. And it comes to the whole root of the problem. And that is the method of operation at the moment, the amount of lands that people have, the social fabric of cane growing and production, is something that is 200 years old. To change it is the only long-term solution. But the pain of changing it, on top of everything else that is going on, is something that in the short term is disastrous.'

The worst-case scenario is that Long Pond will have to close and the sugar economy in Trelawny will collapse. At best, it can survive in a much-reduced form, with mechanical harvesters instead of people in the cane fields, and with the contributions of small (individual) cane farmers excluded from the workings of the estate. Either way, the livelihoods of thousands of people in the parish will be affected, just as the livelihoods of hundreds of thousands across the island as a whole are in jeopardy.

Over the first years of the new century, the sugar economy will have to adjust to the local, and international, conditionalities of sugar production. Below we take a look at its current operation.

The sugar-cane economy

At regular intervals during the day in the months of the crop, an open-topped bus winds its way from the Long Pond cane lands back through the local villages. On board are men and women – the 'field gang' – returning from their shifts in the cane fields. Under the scorching sun the men have been cutting canes which the women have been binding; as they worked they were allowed to take breaks to drink the iced water that is the only extra Long Pond gives them. At midday, a few boiled the water and added flour to make a plain dumpling of flour and water for their lunch. One woman said that she was living just on her iced water because today she could not even afford to buy flour. The ages of the men vary but most of the women are middle-aged or older. One says that she has been working in the cane fields for sixty years, and has nothing to show for it but tough hands. She says she will have to keep on working until she dies.

All the workers on board the bus agree that they are working in the cane fields because their lives have afforded them no other opportunity to provide a survival wage. All talk of the constant hardship they have endured. They are unanimous too, however, in their conviction that if the estate were to close their sufferings would be much, much greater. 'We will be dead out around here if Long Pond is gone' said one 'it will be nothing but ice water every day'.

The sentiments of these cane workers illustrate the development dilemma presented by the continuing survival of the sugar industry in Jamaica and the Caribbean as a whole. They work in the sugar industry because they have no other option, because the industry's very existence has thwarted alternative development. But take the sugar industry away, and in the short run at least their situation becomes even worse. Indeed, this dilemma is woven into the lives of many of those in Gaythorne who struggle to make a living away from the industry. A shortage of alternative employment usually means that in some way they remain dependent upon the sugar economy; a shortage of capital means they are not able to invest in the tools or inputs they need for their small farming or trade activity.

Yet the sugar industry itself pays so badly that even those who work in it full time are still forced to look for extra forms of income.

While some households are entirely reliant upon the sugar-cane economy, most in Gaythorne have to seek diverse sources of support. Of these, the most important are remittances, which – in addition to sugar – provide the primary source of income into the community. Practically every household is also engaged in small farming, whether on a minuscule scale, growing food for their own 'pot', or selling their surplus at market too. In addition, people are involved in a range of trade and service activities. Some young men drive taxis or find intermittent work in the construction industry; a very few men and women have jobs in hotels.

Others are mechanics, shopkeepers, dressmakers, domestic workers or cosmetologists. A common thread amongst these occupations is underemployment. In a poor community like Gaythorne, unemployment is practically a meaningless concept – even those without waged employment are very likely to be involved in subsistence activity, and old age will not provide an exception. Long working hours will rarely equate to adequate pay and so even those in full-time jobs will still seek out other ways in which to make money. Most importantly, much of the employment opportunities afforded by the stagnant rural economy are seasonal, irregular and informal. Therefore a young man may describe himself as a mechanic but actually work full time as a cane cutter during the crop, or a woman may state that she is a hairdresser but in fact not have worked in several months, and be largely dependent upon the earnings of her baby-father who works in the Long Pond sugar factory.

In this way, people manage to sustain themselves, and also sustain the belief that they are moving away from dependence upon the sugar industry. But in reality it remains as a core component of nearly all the households in the community. For the more affluent households and the very poorest, the Long Pond estate is very likely to play a role in their economic maintenance.

It is implicit too in the social stratification of the community, for within the sugar industry itself there are carefully observed pecking-orders: field work is held in the lowest regard, work in the factory is less denigrated, mechanical jobs are more highly regarded and those working in any kind of management role are respected. Within these categories there are nuances, and even different tasks within field work will have different sociocultural connotations. Throughout the sugar industry, the most

Table 2
Sugar in the Caribbean – selected countries

	Hectares cultivated	Number of factories	Number of people employed (direct)	Number of people employed (indirect)
Barbados	10,600	3	3,500	6,000
Jamaica	45,000	8	36,500	15,000
St Kitts	4,000	1	2,400	7,000
Trinidad & Tobago	28,000	2	30,400	11,000

Source: ACP Group aide-memoire on ACP sugar, January 2000

menial and lowly paid jobs are undertaken by women, who weed the cane fields and spread fertiliser and get paid on a daily rate. The exception to this, however, is cane farming, which is not stigmatised. Many canefarmers are women – and households across the socio-economic spectrum are involved in this independent production for sale to the estate.

The stigma of canecutting, however, is such that young men will often go to enormous lengths to hide the nature of their employment, and many cane cutters will even migrate to different parishes to work during the crop. A young man from Trelawny, for instance, may travel to the south of the island for several months to cut canes for Monymusk or Frome estate, rather than work at Long Pond. Similarly, some of the field gang at the Long Pond estate are from different parts of the island. The estate provides 'barracks' – decrepit wooden sheds with bunks – for the migratory field force; the luckier ones are able to rent rooms in Gaythorne or other villages for the crop. Young men living locally are known to hide in the bushes on the way to the fields to change in to their work clothes: 'they na want anyone to know, so they put dem pretty shoes back on before reaching their yard'. And for this reason, it is difficult to gauge just how many people from Gaythorne are dependent upon this type of work. There are considerable discrepancies between the number of people in Long Pond employment, and the numbers who will admit to it. 'Pride' it is said, 'goes before certain types of work.'

There are really two sugar economies in Gaythorne: a 'formal' and an 'informal' one. The central difference between the two is that the former is taxable, while informal activity is able to avoid some aspect of government legislation or control. All of the employment at Long Pond is formal; indeed, given that the mass of work in the rural economy as a whole is unofficial, the estate provides the major form of taxable income from the area. But in addition, a huge informal economy exists around the 2,000 cane farmers who grow canes to sell to the estate.

Most cane farmers do as much of the work as they can themselves in their 'cane piece'. Partners and children help too, and during harvesting children will often miss school. But cane cutting is a labour intensive job and it also has to be done rapidly, and so there is a huge informal network of fieldworkers who can be hired on a daily basis. Young men are more likely to admit to this sort of informal canecutting then they are to working in the estate fields. The stigma of working for the 'independent' man or woman is not so great; also, the small farmer is forced to pay cane cutters more than the estate because the work on offer is so temporary, and because they do not have insurance against injury. Informal field gangs will move from farmer to farmer during the crop, working for each for a day or so as their small patches of cane are cut, tied and transported to Long Pond.

As well as paid employment, a lot of cane farmers share their resources with each other during the crop. Under the 'day-fe-day' system, a farmer will work for a friend for free to help get their canes in, and call in the favour when his or her canes are ready to be cut. Young men who normally eschew field work will join the field gang for their grandfather or aunt; young women will act as 'cook' and prepare curried goat and rice and peas for the workers at midday. Once the canes begin to be cut there is a real sense of urgency. Even the youngest children in Gaythorne understand that getting the canes to the factory becomes a race against time, as the sucrose levels begin to decline immediately after cutting. Hours lost in getting the canes bundled and transported can mean a real loss in annual income for a household. It is this knowledge that unifies the voluntary field gang, but can also leave the small operator open to exploitation by the informal cutters.

Agricultural Association members with machetes, Haiti   *Sean Sprague/Panos Pictures*

The 'formal' sugar economy provides jobs for over a thousand people and as such is the most important official source of employment for Gaythorne people. Some individuals, such as cane cutters, work for Long Pond in the field only during crop, where they may work six or seven days a week for the whole season and get paid according to the amount of canes cut. Others do not 'finish' the crop, but quit as soon as they have managed to make just a little bit of money. Some may work full-time as cutters during the crop and part-time in the fields out-of-crop, again being paid either on a daily basis or by piece work. Others may work only part-time or irregularly on a seasonal basis only. For those involved in transport, payment may be per day, per tonnage hauled, or per trip made.

Around 400 people are employed in the factory. At the factory, cane is first weighed and sampled for juice and quality determination (for the basis of payment). Sucrose is then extracted from the canes by a series of processes which also produce bagasse (or trash, subsequently used as fuel in the boiler house) and molasses (used to produce rum in the distiller). Job specifications in the factory refer directly to the stage of the process at which the individual is employed – they may work, for instance, as a mill feeder, a boiler attendant or a sugar bagger. All employment is paid on a daily basis, but the payment and esteem of the job depends on its level of skill. Long Pond also employs mechanics, security guards and electricians, and people who work in administration, chop wood for the factory furnace or repair the roads into the cane fields. Men are also employed to work in the rum distillery.

Traditionally, there has always been a large 'illicit' economy attached to the Long Pond estate. Granulated sugar from the factory generally finds its way back to Gaythorne. Although sugar is used in large quantities in most households in Gaythorne, it is not for sale in any of the local small shops; it's not really something that has a price attached to it. Petrol, mechanical equipment, fertiliser and field equipment also finds its way into the informal economy. Moreover, the little rum bars in the community sell overproof white rum stored in plastic containers rather than bottles. Some of this comes from the Long Pond distillery but the more favoured variety actually comes from the other sugar estate in Trelawny. This is Hampden rum, known locally as *joncrow batty* (literally, vulture's bottom). The unofficial rights to 'remove' the rums from the distilleries are traditionally accorded to particular individuals who work there. This is a lucrative trade that the management fight but fail to stop. Amongst the workforce, these 'rights', once established, are often passed on from father to son — a small but highly rewarding benefit from an otherwise harsh industry.

Sugar and survival strategies

In Gaythorne, both the nature of individual engagement in the sugar economy, and the form of occupational multiplicity that an individual undertakes varies according to age, gender and family situation. Although the perceived wisdom is that the workforce of the sugar industry is ageing, people of all ages — from school-leavers to ninety year olds — are involved. The majority, however, are over forty years old. A third of these people are women, and their age profile is older still than it is for men. It is certainly the case that it is the young men and women in Gaythorne who are most vociferous in their loathing of the industry, and many elderly people complain bitterly about how the younger generation 'won't go to the bush, because they just want fast work.' And that many young men would prefer

Sugar cane going into the crushing mill, Belize

Chris Sharp/ South American Pictures

to go for very long periods 'sitting on the side of the road' rather than work in a cane field.

But equally, there are cane cutters at Long Pond in their twenties and thirties, and no shortage of young men who are waiting for a job at the factory. Although women in particular do seem to be avoiding work in the industry at any cost, it is a simple fact that there are very few other opportunities afforded by the stagnant rural economy. For those that need to work, the sugar economy is the most likely source of income.

While some elderly people complain that the younger generation 'don't want to mud up them shoes', many parents also want to protect their children from the hardships that they have endured and want to see them have a better life. Some young men and women are therefore supported by their families throughout their twenties as they struggle to set themselves up in a trade or service activity, outside of the sugar industry. It is then in later years, when their ambition has been thwarted by circumstance, and as domestic responsibilities increase, that they will be forced to resort to work in the sugar industry and small farming. Twenty-two year-old Jeff, for example, who was being supported by his family as he tried to make money from 'hustling' tourists and waiting for a chance to 'get foreign', watched an old man set off on a donkey up the steep track to his cane piece, and said 'when mi is his age, that is what mi will be having to do too'.

For young women the story may be a little different. Traditionally in Gaythorne, women have been forced into the cane fields in order to feed their children. Over the last generation, however, and with more widescale international out-migration, things have changed. Many women in Gaythorne still live in poverty, but a good proportion of those with children are getting at least some support through means of a remittance. Most of the remittances that flow into Gaythorne are received by women of child-bearing age. Those still working in the cane fields are therefore those without this support: they are elderly and have relatives overseas, or they are the head of their household, with dependent children and no partner. A third of households in Gaythorne are headed by women and it is generally from this group that the field gang workers come.

As discussed earlier, it is rarely the case that an individual or a household can depend on just a single source of support. This is particularly the case for men – as they age and take on more responsibility, they also struggle to support their households. For women, the pattern differs according to whether or not they are heads of a household. Women with the central responsibility for their households resort to occupational multiplicity, and are also likely to rely too on any income generated by their eldest children. Women who live with their partners tend to be protected from the most extreme poverty and generally do not take on more than one job.

What this means, though, is that many mature adults actually work in the sugar industry in more than one way: they may grow their own cane, and also work full time at the factory; or they may work in the fields at Long Pond, and in the informal sugar economy. This will practically always be combined with the small farming of food for the household to eat – although the best land that the household has access to will have to be devoted to the cane piece. In this way households themselves actually contribute to what George Beckford has referred to as a *plantation bias*.

Because they need the income that cane will earn them, they have to concentrate their farming resources – such as labour and fertiliser – on their cane piece. Their small farming of their 'ground' – for food crops of vegetables, roots and tree crops, for domestic use and for the market – therefore remains under-resourced. What happens within the household can be extrapolated for the parish and for the island itself. Jamaica (and the Caribbean as a whole) is unable to feed itself, and its macro economic problems are heightened by its dependence upon food imports. It starts here, in the hinterland of the sugar industry, and in the short-term perspectives that poor people are forced to adopt within their own maintenance strategies.

This poverty trap is generally only broken through migration. Those who can leave the rural parish for Kingston, or more importantly, who can 'get foreign' for even just a short time, are then able to build up some capital for their return. Those with money can make further money from small farming and cane farming; it is the 'poor man farming', without adequate capital, labour or inputs, that is so denigrated. The advantages of work overseas are so recognised that local politicians are even able to use it as a bargaining tool. Each year thousands of Jamaican men are able to go to the United States on the Farmwork programme, and it is the local politician who decides who gets to go. 'Big men' in Gaythorne, who would never cut cane at Long Pond, will travel to Florida and other southern states on the farmwork programme to cut canes for US dollars. They travel home not just with hard currency but with fridge freezers, CD players and heightened status. In a wider sense, it is not the cane cutting itself that is seen as so contemptuous, but the socio-economic status associated with it when it is undertaken in Jamaica.

Stories of struggle and resistance

Late in the evening during the 'crop', an independent cane farmer sets fire to her cane. 'Breaks' between the cane piece and her 'ground' have been reinforced to control the blaze, and she has waited until the wind has died down. The cane piece burns spectacularly and rapidly, with flames fifteen feet high. In the morning the field gang should arrive to begin cutting the charcoaled cane stalks; a job just a little less arduous than when the piece is 'green' and the entanglement of sharp leaves is almost impenetrable. She hopes the threatened strike at the factory will wait until after her canes have been delivered and processed. If she loses her cane money this year, like last year, then the winter ahead will be really tough.

In the midst of Long Pond lands, an extensive area of mature cane is ablaze. No one is around to control the flames, and it is building up into an inferno that will engulf acres of cane lands. The fire brigade have been called, but will take some time to get here; in the meantime, a few senior personnel from the estate can do little but watch. The workers are on strike and the canes have been sabotaged – the fire an act of defiance that they know will strengthen their hand. For once the canes are burnt they must be cut and processed as soon as possible; with the entire workforce on strike, the estate will carry further losses. Resistance has been as much a part of the sugar industry as struggle – two traditions that define the lives of those living in the sugar areas of Jamaica.

> *'Help me Jesus, cus me suffer bad.'*
> (90 year old man, former cane-cutter)

Mr. Brown suffers the indignities of old age. He is crippled with arthritis, he is deaf, and as a result of glaucoma he is losing his sight. He is bedridden, lying on a bunk in his one-roomed wooden shack. But worst of all, he lives in appalling poverty. Mr. Brown worked as a cane cutter from the age of twelve until he was eighty, never able to earn more than a subsistence salary and never able to build a decent home or save money for his old age.

Without the opportunity to migrate, Mr. Brown spent most of his life in Trelawny working for the smaller sugar estates that eventually amalgamated into Long Pond. Now he lives alone, and survives somehow on a pitiable pension from the sugar industry of just a few dollars a week, and the charity of his neighbours who bring him meals. He cannot afford any medical assistance. The tragedy of Mr Brown's last years epitomises the poverty trap the sugar industry offers to its workforce, and the endless cycle of economic jeopardy. He has been physically unable to leave his yard for the last five years, and living in desperate need since illness forced him to stop work as a canecutter at the age of 83. His greatest sadness is that he can no longer get to church on a Sunday but he mutters his prayers for help constantly.

'The estate, them just rob you and thief you. You can't get no land. Mi grow mi canes and me raise two cow, but mi can't get a start. Them have all the lands and me have to work on a little stony piece'

(woman canefarmer, 58 years old)

Miss Jones has five of her children living at home with her – three of which are in their late teens and early twenties – and two grandchildren. They live in three rooms and although they have water tapped to their yard, they are without an inside toilet. The household manages on the basis of a variety of incomes: two of the adult sons get very occasional work in construction, and the adult daughter gets some support for herself and her children from her baby-father. Miss Jones is the main breadwinner. She has a daughter in Canada who sends her money when she can, and she also farms her ground for food for the household 'pot'. Most importantly, Miss Jones has a two acre cane piece – handed down from her father – which provides the household with its most important source of income. She also works intermittently in the fields of other cane farmers, weeding and fertilising canes out of crop. When she was younger she used to work in the fields at Long Pond, but she says she would have to be 'ready fi dead' before she would do that again.

Miss Jones says her life has been a constant battle to better her position. She wants to increase the amount of cane that she farms but says that Long Pond refuse to give her more land to rent; she also would like to keep some pigs. She applied for an agricultural credit loan to 'start herself up' but was refused. She needs more land to grow her vegetables on but complains that Long Pond has all the best land, leaving her with 'just the stones to dig in'. She wants her 'big lazy boys' to get work to help out, but she does not blame them for not wanting to work in the sugar industry. In fact, she struggles to support them while they try to 'set themselves up in a trade'.

Miss Jones rarely shops in the supermarket in Falmouth. She can only afford to cook one meal a day, and most of that comes from her ground, and from the food trees in her yard. She buys only oil and flour on a regular basis, and in the largest sense is self-sufficient. The household eat meat no more than once a week unless her elder boys are in work, and at the moment she says her youngest daughter is not able to go to school because she does not have any shoes. She can't afford gas to cook on either, but has to send her boys out to bring wood in to build a fire in the yard.

Miss Jones is a Christian and attends church each Sunday; she is waiting for her next life to get her reward for her hard labours in this one.

'I'm proud to say not a single one of my children has put a foot through those factory gates.'

(80 year old man, owner of cane haulage company)

Mr Newton is a content man, enjoying a comfortable retirement. He sits on the veranda of his large brick bungalow and talks about the success that he has been able to make of his life. More importantly, he is very proud of his childrens' achievements. He has five adult children, three of whom are overseas: two are doctors and one a lawyer. One son remains, living in Gaythorne, where he manages a small haulage business that is kept busy during the 'crop', transporting canes to Long Pond. Mr Newton is quick to point out that none of his children have had to work in the cane fields or factory; given his own inauspicious start, this is indeed an achievement.

After leaving school at the age of twelve, Mr Newton worked in the cane fields with his parents. Then, as a young man, he went to the United States to do 'war work'. He returned to Jamaica and Gaythorne at the end of the 1940s with American dollars and big ambitions; his first purchase was a few acres of land for growing cane. Because his time abroad had allowed him to break out of the cycle of poverty that his parents had been trapped in, Mr Newton was able to capitalise on his investment – hiring labour to work in his fields and being able to afford the inputs needed to maximise his yields. Later, he bought the first of many trucks – initially transporting the canes of small farmers and then, as the tourism industry developed on the north coast, hauling building materials and cement mix for the contractors building the hotels.

Mr Newton owns many acres of land around Gaythorne and is a prosperous 'small farmer', growing domestic crops which he sells on at market (he buys most of his food from the supermarket). He employs a large number of casual labourers to work on his ground but he attends – twice a day on his bicycle – to his herd of cows himself for his own enjoyment. Today, he is one of the largest local cane farmers, with nearly one hundred acres, and in addition to the haulage company he owns a couple of houses in the village which he rents out. Unlike most of the inhabitants of Gaythorne, Mr Newton engages in occupational multiplicity not because he has to, but because he can. From his position of advantage he has been able to rely upon the sugar industry to help him increase his wealth, and support his family so that they themselves will not have to fight so hard for socio-economic betterment.

'I'm thinking about my son Jeffrey. I don't work in sugar but his father is a cane farmer. If Long Pond closed then I don't know how he would pay me my maintenance. I'd have to take Jeffrey out of school.'

(30 year old mother of two, part time dressmaker)

Navlette lives with her two young sons in two windowless wooden rooms; she has a water tap in her yard but is without electricity. She has a sewing machine and is a talented seamstress, and works from home as often as she can to bring in some income. In the past, she had great hopes of setting herself up in a successful business and rented a small shop, where she could make clothes and also sell basic groceries. But after a few months she was unable to meet the rent payments and had to abandon her plans.

Navlette gets some irregular support from her baby-father, Delroy; he is quite a 'big man' in the community. Delroy lives with his mother in one of the largest houses in Gaythorne, and Delroy has inherited several acres of canelands from his father. He also was able to 'set himself up' in his late twenties, when he twice went to work in the United States on the 'farmwork' programme. Delroy would never cut canes in Gaythorne, but was delighted to get the chance to cut canes in Florida for US dollars. On his second trip he worked in a fruit canning factory, and again, was able to save foreign currency for his return home.

Although Delroy and Navlette are no longer together, he pays for their oldest son to attend a small private school in Falmouth and provides Navlette with money to feed and clothe the boys. But without her own income, Navlette feels very vulnerable. Navlette is also aware of the jeopardy that Long Pond estate is in. Her mother – now living in Kingston – had worked there in the fields for many years when Navlette and her siblings were young. Her father, who helps her with the boys, still works there as a driver. Navlette knows that her and her boys are ultimately dependent upon the fortunes of the estate and Delroy's cane money. Her greatest fear is that her children, like her, will have to miss out on a good education, and be unable to escape the confines of the community that they were born into.

'The only chance for a little poor boy like me is to dress up nice and hope someone will give me a chance. Mi need to get foreign, so I can come back to Jamaica and get a proper start.'

(23 year old man, on the 'front line')

In the middle of the day in Gaythorne, a group of young men sit by the side of the main road. The same group – give or take three or four – are there most days, sitting in the shade under the trees, chatting up passing women, shouting at or saluting traffic, sometimes smoking ganja. These young men are, in their words, on 'the frontline'; they wear sharp clothes, dark shades and razored haircuts. They do not go to the household 'ground' and do any farming; they never work on a casual basis for local people who need assistance in their fields. Most importantly, they never engage in any way in the sugar industry. Their stance is one of resistance to the constraints that have shaped the lives of their parents and grandparents. They are trying to forge a different way of living, with faster and bigger rewards.

Some of the guys on the roadside have ambitions to 'get a trade'; they want to be carpenters, masons or mechanics. Most of them, though, are looking for something more exciting and immediate. Some of these young men are already on the fringe, or even fully immersed, in criminal activity: selling ganja and cocaine to tourists on the north coast, or involved in robbery or illicit 'scams'. A few might be occasionally employed by local 'big' men who are themselves involved in drug related activity, or are associated with the more dubious side of political activity in Jamaica.

A couple of these 'frontliners' are intimidating and tough, but many are decent young guys. They may be looking in the long term for nothing more than a job as a taxi driver or a barman, or for an American tourist who might want to take them home – but when an economy offers such poor rewards for 'legitimate' activity, they are willing to take up 'illicit' activity when it is offered. In the meantime, their best bet is to sit by the roadside, dressed up to look the part that they want to play, in the hope that an offer will come their way soon. Some will end up in serious gangs, and some will end up heavily immersed in drugs – a few will have violent, premature deaths. And a few might even 'make it', and be able to use the money they save during their more dangerous years to buy a taxi or build a bar and set themselves up in legitimate business, in the meantime helping their mothers and sisters build better homes and lead more secure lives.

Attitudes to the frontliners vary across Gaythorne. To some – especially the elderly – these young men are lazy and vain, branded as criminals with too much pride to do an honest day's work. To others – such as their peer group who *are* working at Long Pond or in farming, they are risk takers and tough men. To a few of the young women in Gaythorne, who famously '*won't talk to no cane cutter because he has rough hands*', they are irresistible, offering a chance for them too to escape the misery of the plantation. Most importantly, however, they offer a vision of how more and more of Gaythorne's youth will be forced to live as the sugar industry collapses, and even less opportunity to pursue a settled life presents itself.

The development dilemma: a local perspective

It is not easy to sum up the dilemma that the sugar industry presents not just for the inhabitants of the community of Gaythorne, but for development planning for Jamaica and the region as a whole. Sugar is an industry in decline in Jamaica, and like other declining industries before it and elsewhere, it is subject to the inevitable tide of history. But this is not the coal industry in the UK in the 1980s, or the infamous 'rust belt' in the United States during the same period. It is much more overwhelming than industrial change or decline in the developed countries of the Europe and North America.

Unlike any other region of the world, the societies of Jamaica and the Caribbean – as chapter four describes – were created for the single purpose of growing sugar. And, as chapter five describes, their subsequent development has been conditioned by the geopolitical conditions that were established through the sugar industry. The very presence of the plantation has prevented Gaythorne, and many other villages like it, from developing a viable domestic agriculture and real alternatives to sugar. At the national level, the economy remains so indebted that it is unable to create any kind of safety net for its citizens. The decline of the sugar industry then, means unprecedented hardship for rural people, for the stagnant local economy offers very few alternative opportunities.

Yet the sugar industry is generally loathed by those who work in it. It is socioculturally unacceptable; for most, it means the trap of endless poverty. And the people of Gaythorne and of rural Jamaica are not a 'peasantry', as sometimes supposed, but are an international labour force with global connections. In the twenty-first century, the industry of the eighteenth century increasingly becomes an anathema. In a globalised world, and for globalised people, the pockets of underdevelopment created and maintained by the sugar industry are more and more obscene.

However, this local level development dilemma is ultimately being resolved at the international level. The conditions of production in Jamaica are in decline, but it is the global arena of geopolitics and commodity trade that is set to make this situation terminal. In the next chapter we explore the complex relationships of trade between the sugar producing countries of the Caribbean and the European and global markets, and the juxtapositioning of the international bodies that negotiate the future of these small island economies. Moreover, we can begin to trace the chains of commodity production that link the poverty of the people of Gaythorne with the sugar consumer in Europe – the connections between the North and South that bond the bag of sugar on the supermarket shelf to the prospects of those who labour in the Long Pond cane fields.

This chapter is based on original research undertaken by the author in 1991, 1992 and 1998.

Chapter Two

Sugar as a Commodity

'There is no region of the world that needs to look more seriously at its role in the 21st Century than the Caribbean. In the post-Cold War era, we have moved beyond the age where trade preferences are the rule and any country that wants to benefit from free trade will have to look very seriously at its economic structure. The train has left the station and the Caribbean nations need to get on board quickly or get left behind.'

Donna Hrinak, (then) US Deputy Assistant of State for Latin America and the Caribbean

About three quarters of all the sugar that is grown worldwide each year is consumed in its country of origin. For the sugar producing islands of the Caribbean, however, sugar was never produced for local purposes. From the beginning, it was grown to be shipped overseas to satisfy the needs of the European colonisers. Today, the region continues to export nearly all of the sugar that it grows; despite thirty years of political independence, the rural economies of these countries remain geared to providing sugar to meet the needs of the developed world.

Sugar, like other agricultural products grown by less developed countries, is traded as a commodity. The pattern of the international trade of commodities has changed little since its establishment in the colonial era, when Europe used its colonies to provide the products that it could not grow itself. World commodity markets are a perennial problem for developing countries that depend on them for their export earnings, as prices are generally very low and typically unstable. Sugar is an extreme case of these problems: not only is the price paid by rich countries to poor countries barely enough to cover the costs of its production, but it also the most variable of any major internationally traded agricultural commodity. Since the early 1980s, prices have been particularly low,

Table 3
Top three exports of selected Caribbean countries

Country	Main Export	2nd	3rd	Main Export %	2nd %	3rd %
Barbados	Cane Sugar	Food Preparations	Electrical components	GBR 100	VEN 59.3 TTO 10.8 SUR 10.7	USA 88.5 GBR 9.7 HKG 0.8
Dominican Republic	Ferro Nickel	Cane sugar	Coffee	BLX 40.7 USA 22.0 KOR 20.0	USA 100	USA 53.4 CAN 12.2 ITA 11.2
Jamaica	Bauxite	Cane sugar	Clothing	CAN 27.5 NLD 21.5 NOR 12.3	GBR 83.1 USA 9.1 FRA 7.9	USA 99.1 CYM 0.3 BRB 0.2
St Kitts & Nevis	Cane sugar	Electrical switches	Electrical parts	GBR 60.1 USA 39.9	USA 100	USA 95.4 ITA 3.0 DEU 1.6

Source: Inter-American Development Bank, 1997
Country codes:

BLX Belgium & Luxembourg	FRA France	NOR Norway
BRB Barbados	GBR Great Britain	SUR Suriname
CAN Canada	HKG Hong Kong	TTO Trinidad &Tobago
CYM Cayman Islands	ITA Italy	USA United States
DEU Germany	KOR Korea	of America
	NLD Netherlands	VEN Venezuela

causing great hardship for those people in poor countries who are reliant upon sugar cane for revenue.

Because of the instability of commodity prices, some special trading arrangements for sugar have evolved. These are certainly not a development panacea and generally benefit the consuming countries more than the producers, but they have at least introduced some price stability for those involved. The European Union buys its sugar from the former colonies of its member states under its Sugar Protocol (formerly of the Lomé Convention), whereby a price is fixed in advance. The USA offers a preferential market to some of its favoured neighbours under its sugar quota system. Other trading relationships have developed out of political affinity between former communist countries.

The Caribbean islands sell their sugar under a range of trading situations: Jamaica sells much of its crop to the European Union, as does Barbados; the Dominican Republic sells some of its sugar to the USA for a guaranteed price but also has to depend upon the world market for its other sugar exports; and communist Cuba, the largest of the Caribbean producers and supported by a guaranteed market for its sugar with the former Soviet Union until the end of communism in 1989, sells its sugar to Eastern European countries and on the world market.

However, within the environment currently developing under the remit of the institutions of global governance – the World Trade Organisation, the World Bank and the International Monetary Fund – special trade arrangements for commodities produced in the South are in jeopardy. Just as these countries were bought into the world economy to function as the producers of raw commodities for the colonisers, now, in the post-colonial period of changing geo-politics and over-supply in the North, their role is no longer clear.

In this chapter, we explore how the system of international trade of commodities has contributed to the underdevelopment of Jamaica and the Caribbean, and look at the evolution of the special trade arrangements that have evolved from their original colonial relationships with Europe. In the case of Jamaica, it is these arrangements that have actually kept the industry alive in the post war period. We consider how the high indebtedness of the region increases its vulnerability to the changing environment of international trade, and consider too the threats to sugar markets also posed from less politically motivated forces, such as artificial sweeteners. Finally, we outline what this means for the Caribbean in the twenty-first century, five hundred years after their first vicious colonial encounter with sugar production. What will the changing role of sugar as a commodity mean for the island economies?

The 'World' Market: a misnomer

On the 'world' market – at its most basic – international trading transactions take place when someone in one country wants to buy sugar that someone in another country has produced. Because sugar is an unusual crop, in that virtually every country in the North and South is both a producer and a consumer, less than a quarter of the sugar that is grown each year is actually traded.

In 1992, for example, 117 million tonnes of raw sugar were produced world-wide and about 21 million tonnes were exported on to the 'world' market. World sugar production for 1997-8 is estimated to be 126 million tonnes raw value and that for 1998-9 to be 128.5 million tonnes. World consumption, conversely, for 1998-9 is estimated at 123.5 million tonnes while world stocks of raw sugar have increased by 1.7 million tonnes. The outlook for 1998-9 is for a large increase in world stocks to 2.3 million tonnes.

Sugar that is not traded under special agreements is sold on the 'world' market at a price that varies according to supply and demand. Between the mid-1950s and the late 1980s, the world sugar price averaged around 16c/lb (at 1985 prices). In 1974, it briefly reached 120 c/lb, and averaged 59c/lb for the year; between 1981 and 1986, the average price of sugar never rose above 8.5c/lb. In 1992 it was just 9c/lb, and at present it is 8.88 c/lb on 23 April 2001. When sugar prices are as low as these, in most years they fail even to cover the production costs of the exporting countries.

Low prices are of little consequence for developed country exporters, such as the European Union, which uses the 'world' market to sell only their excess sugar. And for those Caribbean countries that sell most of their sugar under special arrangements, such as Jamaica and Barbados, their impact is diluted. But for other countries from the region like Guyana or the Dominican Republic, whose economies depend heavily upon revenues from sugar sold on the 'world' market, low prices can spell disaster. It means that the terms of trade – the rate at which exports are exchanged for imports – have moved against the sugar producing country. This has severe social implications. As well as having less money to spend on such things as health and education, or development projects to alleviate poverty, governments also have less money available to buy essential imported goods such as food, or raw materials for other sectors of the economy. For individual families who grow cane or work on plantations, a low price for sugar on the world market means that they may no longer be able to afford to send their children to school or pay the doctor's bill, or even eat dinner. Individual cane farmers, like sugar producing economies as a whole, are locked into a system of having to grow their crop without the knowledge of whether they will actually generate a revenue large enough to cover cost.

Very simply, the price paid for sugar on the 'world' market is determined by supply and demand: when supply is greater than demand, there is a buyer's market and prices are low. The reason why the 'world' market price for sugar is so low and unstable is that the supply of sugar is constantly greater than demand. There are several causes for this. First, historical factors have led to present-day inequalities in the world trading system that have meant that less developed countries remain dependent upon commodities like sugar and therefore have to grow as much of them as they can. Secondly, the special arrangements between some sugar importers and exporters, which guarantee a price higher than that of the 'world' market, allow high-cost production to be sustained in both the North and the South and mean that the supply of sugar is generally higher than it would otherwise be.

Finally, since the 1980s, this over-supply on the 'world' market has been increased both by the expansionist Common Agricultural Policy of the European Union, and attempts by the less developed countries, especially those from the Caribbean and Latin America, to increase revenues from their commodity exports in order to pay the interest on their debts. In reality, the 'world' market is actually the opposite of its name; it is instead the residual market where prices are not inflated or protected by the agricultural superpowers. It does not have a geographical base; rather, commodities that constitute the 'world' market are traded on the commodity markets, in London, New York, Chicago, Singapore and other smaller financial centres.

One of the reasons for the problems surrounding the trade of sugar as a commodity is the nature of the operation of the world/residual market. It is both what economists call 'thin' and 'perfect'. A 'thin' market exists when there is a relatively small number of buyers and sellers; at the same time, the market is 'perfect' when all the buyers and sellers have general and universal knowledge about the product and its price. Because of this, changes in the quantities of sugar traded can have a large impact on its price. The global supply of sugar is able to expand much more quickly in response to a price increase than it is able to contract when prices fall; it is more mobile in the upward than in the downward direction because, as Hagelberg and Hannah explain, there is usually enough 'slack' in the system to expand output quickly in response to attractive prices. Conversely, contraction is more difficult given the heavy capital investment in specialised equipment, and the fixity of assets which is particularly marked in the cane sugar sector because of its perennial crop cycle. Moreover, falling prices mean reduced revenues, and many poor producers have no choice but to increase production in the hope of selling more, thereby making sure that prices fall even further.

The demand response to prices, on the other hand, tends to be skewed in the opposite direction, expanding relatively less in reaction to lower prices than it contracts in response to higher prices. The most obvious reason is that much of the world has reached saturation point in the per capita food demand for sugar. Another reason is that poor importing countries with unsaturated demand may be unable to increase consumption in line with declining prices because of foreign exchange constraints. For their part, importing countries possessing sugar industries have been prone to react to cheaper foreign sugar not by increasing imports but by raising the margin of protection to domestic producers.

The impact of subsidised production on the 'world' market

Mr Brown cuts his canes in Gaythorne with a machete, working under the heat of the Caribbean sun. His knowledge of plant husbandry is great but he is unable to afford the inputs he would like to use to increase his yield. Neither has he been able to afford to replant his cane field in recent years and no amount of his expertise can prevent the sucrose content of his canes from dropping. During the recent drought he was watering his cane piece with a bucket, making endless trips to the tap on the roadside. Even the weeding is done by hand. Mr Brown feels that everything is stacked against him; it's no wonder his return on his land is decreasing year on year.

Mr Brown, on his arable farm in East Anglia, climbs into his tractor on a warm spring morning on the tarmacked yard of his farm and turns on the air conditioning. As he cranks smoothly into gear and heads out along the drive towards his sugar beet fields, he picks up his mobile to call his foreman to check on the day's activities. He wants to take a look at his 100 acre plus of sugar beet that was planted a few weeks ago; they'll need to start spraying tomorrow and he wants to remind himself of how many men and machines he needs on the job.

Unlike his father, Mr Brown is an affluent man. Farming has changed a lot for his generation. The farm had been a very different place when he was a boy – well, it had actually looked like a farm! Nowadays it is all advanced machinery and grain silos, and the hedgerows and trees have slowly been removed from the fields to make way for greater returns. He couldn't complain though – he'd made a lot of money over the last twenty years and was going to be retiring soon. Of course, the prospects for the future weren't so good, with the imminent cutbacks in subsidies from the Common Agricultural Policy. He was glad he wasn't coming into the business today. But he'd been able to run a profitable business and he and his wife were looking forward to reaping some of the rewards of years of hard work; in fact, she was already planning a world cruise. ·

Within an environment of international rivalry and protectionism, the international trade of sugar has been conditioned by unstable market characteristics and over-supply since the early colonial period. When the sugar trade evolved from the colonisation of the Caribbean islands by the British, for instance, it was known as 'white gold' because of the wealth that it created. Other countries wanted their share of the profits, and by the middle of the nineteenth century, new plantation territories in Cuba, Brazil, Mauritius and the East Indies had been developed.

At the same time, a highly protected and subsidised beet sugar industry was being promoted in the North to alleviate the depressed state of European agriculture. The consequent 'over-supply' of the product on the world market caused prices to plummet and brought the British Caribbean sugar industry to the brink of collapse. This situation has largely continued to the present, and the sugar-cane producers of the Caribbean and other less developed regions of the world are still living with the legacy of historical inequalities in the trading system, as they face continuing 'unfair' competition from beet sugar grown in the North.

Since the early 1980s this competition has had an unprecedented impact on the condition of the world sugar market, as the agricultural policies of the developed countries, and particularly those of the European Union, have transformed the beet sugar industry. In 1967 the countries which now comprise the European Union imported nearly four million tonnes of cane sugar between them. By the mid 1980s they were *exporting* nearly four and a half million tonnes of beet sugar, largely onto the world market to be traded by commodity brokers around the world and purchased by sugar importing countries. The particular stagnation of the world market price from the beginning of that decade is largely attributed to this development, together with the expansion in sugar exports from, and the reduction in sugar imports to the United States of America.

The European Union's sugar policy is part of the Common Agricultural Policy, which was established in 1958 with the signing of the Treaty of Rome by the Union's founding members. The agricultural policy that was applied commonly to the member states was devised in response to the serious food shortages that had been experienced throughout Europe during and after the Second World War. The founding group of countries decided that food security was vital and that this could best be achieved by self-sufficiency. They decided, therefore, to devise an agricultural policy that could make farming attractive. This policy applied to a wide range of agricultural sectors such as dairy products, meat and cereals, as well as sugar.

The central tenet of the European Union's Common Agricultural Policy is that it guarantees minimum prices for European farm produce. Once a year, Farm Ministers from each of the member states meet to agree how much will be paid for each agricultural product for the year to come. Over the last fifteen years, the price received by European farmers for their sugar has generally been *three to four times* higher than that on the world market. Farmers, therefore, have been encouraged to produce vast quantities of sugar along with beef, dairy products, cereals and wine, and have, in fact, therefore produced far more than could be consumed in Europe. During the 1980s, while the famous 'lakes' of milk and 'mountains' of butter built up in Europe, the world market became the dumping ground for about a third of the sugar that the Union's beet farmers produced every year.

Even though the average cost of producing beet sugar is as much as fifty per cent higher than the average cost of producing cane sugar world-wide, European farmers saturate their domestic market with beet sugar in place of the cane sugar that the Union would otherwise import. Then the surplus from this production, which would not be viable without subsidies, is sold on the world market at prices with which poor cane farmers cannot compete. Moreover, because European consumers have to pay higher prices for their agricultural produce and heavier taxes in order to support the CAP, their demand for sugar is suppressed and this lowers world market prices even more.

Estimates of the long-term effect of the EU regime on the world price range from 5% to 17.5%, and the foreign exchange costs to developing countries which export on the world market are substantial.

The world market for sugar is further distorted by the trade and agricultural policies of other major developed countries – particularly the

United States – and the protectionist policies of countries such as India and China, who are largely self-sufficient in sugar but guard their industries from competition by protectionist barriers. These policies mean that a large volume of production is maintained even when its cost is far above the world market price. When necessary, governments will also subsidise the exports of surplus sugar to be sold on the world market. The net result is a compounding of the artificially low world market prices paid for sugar, which fluctuates to a higher price only in the short-term when the harvests of the major producers are damaged by climatic catastrophes. This state of affairs is disastrous for those poor sugar exporters, like the Dominican Republic or Guyana, who cannot afford to protect or subsidise their industries in the same way.

The trade trap

The low price paid for sugar as a commodity is the consequence of the historical evolution of the international trading system that is explained in chapter four. With Caribbean sugarcane at its centre, the system allowed the colonial powers to increase their economic wealth at the expense of the poor countries which they 'owned', and used to produce the goods that they wanted. Until the present, and despite the end of colonialism, the pattern of international trade has continued to increase the economic power of the developed countries – who have little desire to change the status quo – and has reproduced the inequality in wealth between North and South. As Kevin Watkins writes in *Fixing the Rules*:

'because of their trading power, rich countries can ensure that they pay a low price for the goods that poor countries sell... they are also able to make it very difficult for poor countries to diversify their economies and develop manufacturing industries to enable them to sell more expensive goods, like those that the North produces, or even refine their own raw materials themselves. The industrialised countries, for instance, make a charge known as a tariff against poor countries if the sugar they sell to them is refined rather than raw... This means that the sugar-producers are discouraged from developing their own refining industries that have the potential to create employment and generate wealth. Instead, the poverty of commodity dependent economies means that they have little option but to carry on selling their raw agricultural products, whilst experiencing continually worsening terms of trade, in order that they may be able to purchase essential imports.'

This situation, in which poor sugar producing countries like those of the Caribbean find themselves, is known as the 'trade trap'. It explains why poor countries keep growing sugar to sell internationally, even though it appears not to be in their best interests to do so. It also ensures that the theoretical benefits of trade to less developed countries, as commonly espoused by the North, can not be realised.

International trade, economists generally agree, should be mutually beneficial to trading partners if they specialise in producing goods for which they have a particular advantage – a belief that has evolved from the theory of comparative advantage, generally credited to the nineteenth century economist David Ricardo. The theory states that output and the increases from specialisation and exchange will be maximised when each country or region specialises in the production of goods and services in which its comparative advantage is largest. For a variety of reasons, a particular country may be able to produce something cheaper and better than others: Country A may be able to make its own watches, but Country B can make them cheaper and of the same quality. It may pay Country A to buy watches from B, and for A to concentrate on making those goods in which it has an advantage over B – and then for A and B to exchange goods. But, whatever the theory may be, the economic growth of the North has failed to 'trickle down' to the South. The Caribbean countries may well have some comparative advantage in sugar production – with their fertile soils and climatic conditions ideally suited to growing cane – but 400 years of this type of industry have failed to deliver any real economic benefits.

The debt trap

The sugar producing countries of the South do not just need the revenue generated by commodity trade to pay for imports; they also need to pay the interest on their debts. For the last two decades the spectre of debt has contributed the final factor in the low price equation of sugar as a commodity, and has been a compounding influence on the underdevelopment of primary commodity dependent nations. Not only has debt increased the hardship experienced by the poorest people; it has also conditioned the way in which national sugar industries are managed.

Most poignantly, it works the other way round too in a cyclical fashion – it is the state of underdevelopment that commodity dependence brings that in turn sets the conditions for the debt problem. To understand this conundrum, and what it means for the sugar industries of the Caribbean, it is necessary to first explore the rise of international debt in general, and the role that the institutions of global governance have in managing it.

The second half of the twentieth century saw the creation of the first consequential institutions of global governance: the United Nations, the International Monetary Fund, the World Bank, and the General Agreement on Tariffs and Trade (GATT). Ideas for post-war multilateral economic co-operation focused on two main areas: monetary and financial institutions to deal with the problems of exchange rates, currency stabilisation, reconstruction finance and international investments; and a trade organisation to deal with the problems of commercial policy and to promote the liberalisation of trade. The former led to the Bretton Woods Conference and the establishment of the International Monetary Fund and the World Bank (International Bank for Reconstruction and Development); the latter to the Havana Charter embodying the scheme for an International Trade Organisation, which never saw the light of day. Instead, a more limited scheme for trade liberalisation, the GATT, was put into effect. As Nassau Adams writes:

> 'this was very much an Anglo-American affair... It goes without saying that the influence of the underdeveloped countries on these negotiations was nil or negligible. ...As originally conceived, both the Fund and the Bank were to play a major role in restoration of economic equilibrium after the war... but in the immediate aftermath of the war what was needed was assistance for reconstruction. And while the Bank made an early start in fulfilling its role, it quickly became apparent that the resources at its disposal were far short of what was needed... A major shift in American policy... led to the launching of the 'Marshall Plan'... The Bank was thus sidelined...'

For the Bank, whose main purpose was to be reconstruction financing, very soon turned instead to development financing of less developed countries – largely for the development of their public utilities.

During the 'modernisation' development era of the 1960s, large-scale development projects were funded across the Third World – this was a period of great optimism for the development project as a whole, and many poor countries experienced substantial growth rates and improvements in infrastructure, public health and literacy. But following the 'oil shock' in the early 1970s, and the steep increase in the price of petroleum, poor countries began to borrow heavily – from private international banks as well as the World Bank – in order to keep up growth rates and import substitution programmes. Moreover, with burgeoning populations and strengthening middle classes, money was also needed to prop up the balance of payments for those poor nations becoming increasingly dependent upon imported foods. But by the beginning of the early 1980s, balance of payments problems for the biggest international debtors became critical; debt had grown to such an extent that interest payments alone were greater than the annual GDP of many debtor countries. Many countries had borrowed at low interest rates during the 70s, but by the 80s interest rates increased sharply. In 1982, Mexico started an international banking crisis when it actually defaulted on its interest payments.

It was a long road that the International Monetary Fund had taken from the original conception in the minds of the American and British Treasury officials, who sought an institution that could provide temporary liquidity to ease the pains of adjustment to balance of payments disequilibrium, to its present role of debt-collector on behalf of private banks. The IMF became synonymous with Structural Adjustment, which has become standard fare in the policy matrix of debtor countries. The Structural Adjustment Loans programme was introduced in 1980 as a form of Bank lending geared to the realisation of specific policy changes and institutional reforms.

The Caribbean region as a whole is one of the most heavily indebted in the world, and the resulting debt-service obligations, aggravated by high interest rates, absorb much of the poor countries' export earnings. The poverty associated with its reliance upon sugar as a commodity has contributed to the region's debt; money was also borrowed to fund import substitution and attempts to diversify the economies away from their plantation base. The region's balance of payments difficulties have been enhanced by its need to import food, which as chapter one explained, is also associated with the dominance of sugar plantations on the best agricultural land. Structural adjustment, however, rather than assisting in diversification away from the root cause of their problem, has actually increased the importance of sugar industry to the debtor islands, and encouraged them to increase their output in order to meet their interest payments.

Under the auspices of structural adjustment, for example, poor Jamaicans have become even more impoverished. As exchange rates have collapsed, inflation in the price of basic foodstuffs has been rampant; as spending on public utilities and services has been reduced, education and health services have declined. In Gaythorne, for instance, farmers have dug up recreational land in an attempt to become more self-sufficient in food. Under structural adjustment, Long Pond, and the other state owned sugar estates, have been forcibly privatised, and the industry as a whole encouraged to increase its output and sales on the world market. But this prescription is uniform, and debtor nations everywhere are encouraged to expand their commodity production. As with rubber, tin, or cocoa, so with sugar – the more that is produced, the greater the fall in price, and the less value it provides to the producer nation. Thus the more contradictory the international governance of trade policy becomes.

International agreements and special trading relationships

For their benefit (and perhaps to their credit), the developed nations have attempted to introduce some order into the international sugar trade, and develop methods of commodity trade that avoid the 'world' market. From first to last, international sugar agreements have been very much children of their time. The world's first multilateral inter-governmental commodity agreement, which attempted to stimulate the production of beet sugar in Europe, was signed in Paris in 1864; this was shortly followed by attempts, from the beginning of the twentieth century, to improve the market conditions for cane sugar from the colonies. Since then, two different types of arrangements, designed to ameliorate price instability, have evolved. The first of these are the various International Sugar Agreements that, over the last fifty years, have been applied to the world sugar market. These have not met with great success. The second are special trade arrangements between countries, either in a bilateral sense or between larger trading groups.

There is no doubt, as the later discussion will explain, that colonial 'guilt' has played a role in the development of special trade arrangements for cane sugar, between Europe and the Caribbean. Over time, indeed, this 'guilt' has moved from being carried by individual colonial powers to a collective sense of responsibility on the part of the European Union. While cane, in the modern era, is a colonial legacy maintained by the burden of historical circumstance, beet has been viewed as a capitalist venture. Importantly, however, there appears to be less and less room for the former in the world economy of the future.

The very first international commodity agreements were based around sugar, and began as early as 1864 when, at the Paris Sugar Convention, the governments of the UK, Belgium, France and the Netherlands gathered to consider ways in which they could aid the European sugar beet industry in order to stimulate the depressed agricultural sector. They decided, in the interests of their treasuries, to put their sugar industries on an equal competitive footing between them using agreed subsidies, known as Continental Bounties. By the end of the century, however, the agreement had failed. The European sugar industries had matured and governments of exporting countries had grown tired of escalating subsidies. Moreover, Britain had acquired in Mr Joseph Chamberlain a Secretary of State for the colonies, who had at one time invested in the West Indies and was familiar with West Indian problems. He became convinced that the Continental Bounties were the cause of the severe economic problems of the British Caribbean colonies and that some defence of their interests was necessary. Chamberlain set up the West India Royal Commission which, when it reported in 1897, was unanimous in urging the British Government to convince the continental countries to abandon the bounties.

In 1902 at the Brussels Convention, the governments of Austria, Belgium, France, Germany, Hungary and Italy, the Netherlands, Norway, Spain, Sweden and the UK agreed, under the Brussels Treaty, to phase out the various systems of bounties on beet sugar. This agreement was extended in 1908 and 1912, until it was rendered inoperative by the First World War and formally annulled in 1920. While it had provided some relief to the British West Indian sugar industries that were in a state of almost total collapse, it was actually the destruction of the European beet industry by war that provided a more substantial boost to the fortunes of the colonies. In fact, the history of the Brussels Convention foreshadowed the experience of subsequent international sugar agreements. It was possible for governments to agree common aims and intentions, and set out how best they could be achieved. But it was difficult to alter the basic economic conditions that governed excess world sugar production and the consequent fall in its market price.

In 1937 the International Sugar Organisation was established, with an agenda to promote co-operation in matters relating to sugar, and with a quest for market stability. To this end, in the same year, the first of nine International Sugar Agreements was implemented. The agreement established export quotas for its members and included provisions relating to national stocks of sugar. It also set a price objective, defined as 'a reasonable price, not exceeding the cost of production, including a reasonable profit, for efficient producers'.

Before its success or otherwise could be ascertained, the economic provisions of the 1937 agreement had to be suspended on the outbreak of the Second World War. The four subsequent agreements containing economic provisions (implemented in 1953, 1958, 1968 and 1977) were unable to secure any form of stability on the world market. The more sugar became an article of mass production and consumption, the more it grew in political and strategic relevance, and the less inclined national governments were to regard international market regulation as anything other than supplementary to domestic controls.

All attempts at market regulation were finally abandoned when the 1977 agreement, which had established export quotas for its members at times of over-supply, was rendered completely obsolete by the behaviour of the European Community who had refused to join the Organisation. While the quotas in 1978 and 1979 had lowered the exports of the member states (of the Organisation) by some two million tonnes, the EC used the opportunity to encourage an expansion of its own production and exports. This resulted in the collapse of the agreement in 1984, when world prices fell by 30%. Since then, ISAs have included administrative provisions only. In effect, the free market has been unregulated for the greater part of the last fifty years and nations have relied more on domestic than international means of stability.

In essence, as Hagelberg and Hannah write, international sugar agreements have addressed the problem of supply side management by a combination of quantitative regulation and stockholding. Applied to sugar, supply management to stabilise prices in the first instance involves smoothing crop fluctuations of considerable magnitude, for which sugar is not very suitable, at least at the global level. Moreover, sugar is a high-volume product of relatively low unit value. At free market prices, raw sugar has often been cheaper than rice or soybeans. Moreover, though storable, raw sugar is subject to deterioration. Consequently, stocks of the magnitude required for international price stabilisation would present serious physical and financial problems. By way of comparison, the International Cocoa Agreement of 1980 provided for a buffer stock of up to 250,000 tonnes, the International Natural Rubber Agreement of 1979 a buffer stock of 550,000 tonnes, whereas the International Sugar Agreement of 1977 required exporting members to accumulate 'special stocks' of 2.5 million tonnes.

The second type of agreement that has been designed to circumvent the vicissitudes of the 'world' market relates to the special trading arrangements between particular countries. These began in 1951 with the British Commonwealth Sugar Act, which offered a guaranteed price and market for a quota of sugar from a favoured country. Since then, other special arrangements have evolved to shape much of the world's trade in sugar.

As mentioned above, there is no doubt that colonial obligation played an important role in the establishment of such agreements. However, while the colonisers maintained access to their own markets for cane sugar, they maintained the constraints upon the Caribbean sugar industry that had been there from the start. They would buy raw sugar only; the refining (the value-added part of the sugar industry) was to be done in Europe, and the Caribbean would not be encouraged to develop its industry into the areas where more profit potentially lay.

When Britain joined the European Community in 1973, the commitment to its former colonies under the Commonwealth Sugar Act was renegotiated to produce a Community-wide pact including the former colonies of other member states – known as the Sugar Protocol of the Lomé Convention – that ensured that neither the UK's refining interests nor its cane suppliers would be disrupted. The Sugar Protocol guarantees Caribbean producers, along with other African and Pacific Rim countries, a regular outlet for a fixed quota of sugar at the same price as that received by European beet farmers. This is currently about three times the world price.

Since 1975, the Lomé Convention has been the main basis of the development co-operation between what are now the EU and the majority of the African, Caribbean and Pacific Rim states (ACP). The latter now number 71 including 75% of the world's least developed countries. The convention provides a framework of preferential tariffs and quotas, and special protocols (annexes that do not cover all ACP states) for particular commodities, including sugar, bananas, beef and rum. Lomé also provides humanitarian aid, finance for development projects, as well as structural adjustment deals that trade debts for economic reform. It has a political dimension too, promoting democracy, human rights, and the rule of law.

It is important to note that, at the time that the Lomé Convention was being negotiated, the benefits of such arrangements were not automatically presumed by the Caribbean islands. In Jamaica, for example, the negotiations for access coincided with a national controversy (which came to be known as the 'Great Sugar Debate'), filling the pages of the *Daily Gleaner*.

This debate was at the heart of the Caribbean's focus on the generation of an indigenous development perspective, which chapter five explores in detail. In short, the government of the island, and representatives of the sugar industry, felt it was a matter of 'life and death' that the colonial preference that had been granted to Jamaica from Britain was maintained by the EU when Britain joined. Meanwhile, the university academics argued that the now independent Jamaica was better off, in the longer term, without a sugar industry at all and that the continued trade relationship did little but reinforce the nature of the island's dependency. In the end of course, the Lomé Convention was ratified and the special trade arrangement was maintained – the consequences of which we can see today.

The second major special trade arrangement emanates from the USA, which first established a quota system for sugar in the 1930s. Today the US imports varying amounts of sugar from favoured countries – particularly the Caribbean, Central and South America and the Philippines. Its sugar policy, like that of the EU, is based on a commitment to achieve self-sufficiency, stability in supplies and protection to domestic refiners. The US, however, is not laden with the post-colonial obligations of the EU, and does not, therefore, offer the same degree of protection from the vagaries of the market to its suppliers. The quotas afforded to countries like the Dominican Republic and Jamaica have varied significantly since the 1970s and, when domestic producers need to be protected (as happened in 1977 and 1978 when world prices declined) are abandoned altogether. The US has a policy to keep its domestic sugar prices high, and the price paid to its quota holders is at present roughly twice that of the world market.

Bilateral trading agreements

It is certainly the case that special trading arrangements of a bilateral nature have been extremely important for the survival of poor countries' sugar industries. The Jamaican industry for example, like that of other former British territories in the Caribbean, would not have survived the post-war period without the Commonwealth Sugar Act of 1951. Assured of a continuous access for fixed quantities of sugar to the British market at 'a reasonable price to efficient producers', production and exports increased annually in Jamaica at an average of 10% throughout the 1950s.

Special trade arrangements benefit the Caribbean and other poor sugar exporting countries in that they provide a regular source of much-needed revenue; they help to maintain industries upon which millions of rural people depend and indeed, have certainly saved the sugar plantations of Jamaica and Barbados from complete collapse. But while they offer protection from the abysmally low prices paid for sugar on the world market, they still fail to provide the kind of money necessary for governments to diversify the economies of their countries, or the people who toil on the plantations a wage that is above the barest subsistence. While the high cost producers of the Caribbean, whose processing facilities are generally old and poorly maintained because of financial constraints, are kept in business by the preferential markets that their colonial history has afforded to them, they remain trapped within the perpetual poverty of primary commodity dependent trade.

As the Catholic Institute for International Relations explains, the EU provides preferential access to its markets for developing country exports in order to facilitate the smooth and gradual integration of the developing countries into the world economy – one of the EUs stated objectives. In terms of achieving this goal, trade preferences have performed inconsistently. A few countries with the most generous preferential access to the EU market have succeeded in expanding and diversifying their export sector. For example, Mauritius used some of its revenue from exports under the Lomé Sugar Protocol to finance new manufacturing industries, including the clothing export sector which also benefits from preferential access to the EU market. But the vast majority of ACP countries remain heavily dependent on primary commodity exports and have actually seen their share of the EU market decline over the past 20 years through inefficiency. At the same time, many ACP countries remain highly dependent on exporting to the EU market, particularly those that benefit under one of the Lomé commodity protocols.

But ultimately, despite questions over their performance, EU trade preferences appear to have worked in some cases; even those countries that have seen their share in world trade decline might have fared worse without preferential access to the EU market. Arguments for the removal of trade preferences, on the grounds that they have had only limited impact, ignore how damaging this would be to developing countries that have benefited from them. Such arguments also fail to take into account their significance in terms of a political commitment to assist developing countries.

Bitter prospects for the Caribbean sugar trade

Chapter one described the development dilemma inherent in sugar production, as it has touched the lives of the people of Gaythorne. The nature of commodity trade is such that for poor people it has offered little more than a poverty trap; while, at the same time, the system of plantation production has thwarted development and thus led to stagnant rural economies offering few alternative means of survival. However, this dilemma looks set to be resolved by the outcome of overlapping international policy developments which will reduce the price paid for sugar, and ultimately challenge the legitimacy of special trade arrangements *per se*. As we have seen, Jamaica's sugar industry, for example, would be unable to survive if it was forced to depend upon the world market; over the first decade of the next millennium, with the erosion of EU protection, the sugar industries of the Caribbean are likely to slip into terminal decline.

Both the special trade arrangements offered by the Sugar Protocol of the Lomé Convention and the US Quota System are currently being eroded. This 'crisis' is the result of several overlapping policies. Firstly, those countries which supply the EU are expected, from 2000 onwards, to experience a significant fall in the price that they receive for their sugar, as a consequence of the reform of the Common Agricultural Policy. Secondly, the US Quotas are likely to continue the trend of recent years and shrink further, as American food manufacturers gradually replace natural sugar in their foods with cheaper artificial alternative sweeteners, and American agricultural lobbies push for increased access to foreign markets at the next round of WTO negotiations. Both the guilt-laden trade of sugar cane, and the heavily supported beet enterprise of the Union, are under attack in this sense.

The excesses of the CAP which have damaged the world market price for sugar have also placed a heavy burden on the European consumer and taxpayer. During the 1980s, as over-production in many different agricultural sectors went unchecked, the ludicrous nature of Europe's farming policies was challenged both at home and abroad. Pressure from within the Union to cut spending was finally heeded in the late 1980s, when attempts at reform, aimed at cutting back subsidies and lowering levels of production, were introduced. Even more important, however, have been international pressures to curtail European agricultural subsidies. In the 1980s, spiralling exports led the EC into conflict with the US, as the two agricultural superpowers competed for export markets by offering bigger and bigger export subsidies. Together with pressure inside the EC to reduce the cost of the CAP, this farm trade war put reform of the CAP onto the agenda of the world trade talks known (previously) as the General Agreement on Tariffs and Trade, now renamed as the World Trade Organisation.

The WTO is the multilateral forum by which international trading policy is discussed and implemented. It was one of the array of institutions – alongside the IMF and World Bank – to emerge out of the post-war consensus for the need for international economic co-operation and it provides the only set of agreed rules by which trade takes place. These are broadly based upon the Ricardian theory of comparative advantage, and set out to maximise free trade within the international system. Under the WTO, trading rules are discussed and renewed in *Rounds*, named after the country in which they began. There have been eight of these in all: the seventh, the Tokyo Round, lasted from 1973 to 1978, and the last – the Uruguay Round – began in 1986 and was finally agreed, or *ratified* in December 1993. The current round and the ensuing Seattle riots, began in 1999. However, the time lag is such that the ramifications of agreements made during the Uruguay Round will 'kick in' over the next few years; they will be reinforced by the outcome of the next round of talks.

The international sugar trade was almost completely irrelevant to the negotiations of the Uruguay Round of the GATT. Much of international sugar trade is carried out among countries that are not members of the GATT; for example, Cuba, and some countries of the former Soviet bloc and China. Other major sugar producers, although GATT members, are developing countries and therefore face smaller obligations as a result of the Agreement. The overall agricultural excesses of the CAP, and especially the highly subsidised over-production of wheat, were not irrelevant however, and by the time the Agreement was finally ratified, the EU had agreed to curtail its spending on agriculture and reduce its subsidies to farmers.

In July 1997, the EU published its proposals for its framework beyond the year 2000. The package of proposals, known as 'Agenda 2000', includes the European Commission's outline recommendations for further reform of the CAP – required to meet the challenges of EU enlargement, the EU's GATT Uruguay Round commitments to reduce the levels of subsidised exports, the next round of multilateral agricultural trade began at the WTO in 1999, and EU budgetary pressures. As a result, European farmers will experience a reduction in the price that they receive for their sugar beet over the next few years. Under the Sugar Protocol of the Lomé Convention the sugar producers of the ACP countries receive the same price as European farmers for their produce – which means they will also experience a fall in their revenues. The Jamaican Sugar Industry Authority, for example, is now finally acknowledging the inevitability of gradual price decline over the next five years.

In addition to price decline, the Sugar Protocol – the very basis of the special trade arrangement upon which much Caribbean sugar trade depends – is itself in jeopardy. The Lomé Convention – the umbrella under which the Protocol performs – was officially replaced in 2000 by a new ACP/EU partnership arangement, although this will not be ratified until 2002. Unlike Lomé, the Protocol that governs the sugar trade is said to be 'indefinite', and on this basis the ACP countries are refusing to contemplate its decay. However, the *realpolitik* suggests that the post-Lomé, and post-Protocol future is already being drawn up by EU bureaucrats.

In 1998 for instance, the WTO ruled that the banana protocol of the Lomé Convention was inconsistent with its rules, leaving the EU with the problem of how to comply with the ruling within a 'reasonable' period of 15 months, and the ACP banana industries with the problem of how to survive. The banana regime was successfully challenged in the WTO by the USA, supported by Ecuador, Guatemala, Honduras, and Mexico. The

EU appealed, but the WTO's Appellate Body confirmed the Panel's judgement. Although the basic principles of the Lomé Convention are intact until 2002, there are increasing doubts about their shelf life for many years beyond that date.

Since the 1995 mid-term review of the Lomé extended the Convention's fourth term until 2000, doubts about its shelf-life for many years beyond that date have increased. Since November 1996, when the EU Green Paper on options for replacing Lomé appeared, EU and ACP representatives have been engaged in a lengthy process of establishing negotiating positions before a new deal is conducted in 2000. But geopolitics have changed greatly since the Lomé's inception in the 1970s. As the US Secretary of State at the time asserted, in the post-Cold War period the time for special trade arrangements is over; neither the US nor the EU need to buy allegiance. As the US Secretary of State at the time asserted, in the post-Cold War period the time for special trade arrangements is over; now that the communist vs capitalists war is over, neither the US nor the EU need to buy allegiance to their side. Moreover, as the EU has expanded to include members who are without a former 'Empire', the driving force of colonial 'guilt' is also diluted. And indeed, within the rules of the WTO the nature of special protocols can actually be ruled as illegal. In a world of global competition, access to Europe's market is more than valuable. As with bananas, other sugar producing poor countries who are not ACP members are likely to join forces with the US to improve their own economic prospects.

The weakness of the ACP economies means that they are ill-equipped to take advantage of any new export market opportunities that the WTO agreements may provide in other sectors. Losses from reduced sugar revenues will therefore not be offset by gains in another sector. Under the constraints of structural adjustment and debt repayments, they are forced into reliance upon commodity exports and are unable to access the capital needed to diversify their economies to meet the needs of the new world trade agenda. The scenarios for the short-term future are not positive; but it is clear that the post-sugar destiny for the Caribbean is dawning. The rhythms of the cane crop that have provided the backdrop to life in Gaythorne, and in other sugar communities throughout the Caribbean will finally be eroded.

Saccharine sweet: sugar alternatives

On a global scale, sugar as a commodity also faces another threat. High prices in developed countries, together with increased diet-consciousness, have encouraged the development of 'alternative' and 'artificial' sweeteners. In the EU their production and sale is restricted in order to protect sugar producers, but in the US it is not, and the policy of keeping domestic sugar prices high has encouraged their production. The most important in the world sweetener market are high fructose-corn syrup (HFCS) made from maize, and low-calorie high intensity sweeteners, such as saccharin and aspartame. Alternative sweeteners together constitute about 18% of world sugar/sweetener annual production.

Artificial sweeteners of the chemical variety have a long and chequered history. In 1879, while developing new food preservatives, a young John Hopkins chemistry research assistant accidentally discovered that one of the organic compounds he was testing was intensely sweet. He named it saccharin, after *sakcharon*, the Greek word for sugar and it became a sweetener for diabetics and the weight conscious – who soon learned that it had the same calorific properties as sugar. Saccharin was banned in the early 1900s, then restored during the sugar shortage years of World War One and remained popular through World War Two. By the 1960s, with no other artificial noncalorific sweetener available, saccharin use soared and Americans were using 2,500 tons of saccharin a year, mostly in soft drinks.

Today, Britain has banned saccharin (except as an at-table sugar substitute) and France permits its use only by prescription. Since 1977, because of suspected links with cancer, it has carried health warnings in the US. In 1981, however, *aspartame* (commonly branded as Nutrasweet) was approved for use as an artificial sweetener, and today it has largely replaced saccharin. Aspartame was also discovered by accident, in 1965, and is now found in breath mints, milk drinks, multivitamins, yoghurt, cereals and sugar-free chewing gum.

The trajectory of maize-based sweeteners has been rather different. While the production costs of HFCS are generally more than the price of sugar on the world market, their price in the US is about half of that of sugar. HFCS production has been increasing over time and the US now accounts for 72% of world HFCS consumption. The 1984 decision by PepsiCo and Coca-Cola to use HFCS in their drinks had a critical impact upon quota holding countries. In the Dominican Republic, for example, by 1990, four sugar mills had been closed and thousands of sugar workers were without jobs. As the trend towards artificial sweeteners is set to continue, further cuts in the US quotas are likely.

Sugar as a commodity for the Caribbean islands

As we saw in the last chapter, the role of sugar as a commodity has done few favours for the people of Gaythorne; and, more widely, it has done little for the Caribbean region as a whole. Indeed, the nature of international trade is such that its benefits have never been equally shared, and the producers of primary commodities have generally been relegated to the bottom rung of the international economic order. Special trade arrangements have failed to remove this basic inequality; rather they have allowed inefficient sugar producers to stay in business so that the plantations may provide a survival wage to their workers, and the national economies can maintain their interest payments on the debt owed to the international bankers. Moreover, it is the poverty associated with commodity production that has actually created this debt, while the constraints of structural adjustment mean that there is little capital available for investment to create more efficient and competitive industry. Sugar as a commodity has tied the Caribbean into a contradictory and negative set of rules.

In many ways, this set of rules has developed outwards from the Caribbean region. The development of sugar as a commodity, and as a global foodstuff, began four hundred years ago in the Caribbean islands; the European industrial revolution and the development of the modern world economy were both driven by the wealth that the Caribbean generated for its colonisers. The colonial 'guilt' that hastened the Lomé Convention into being was generated by a very long and important history. In chapters four and five we explore this history, from the first colonial encounter until the present. What are the circumstances that have led to the desperate struggles experienced by those in Gaythorne? What attempts have been made during the twentieth century to diversify the Caribbean economies away from sugar? Through exploring this history we will better understand the connections between the Caribbean, Europe and the US, and consider the possibilities that lie ahead for the political economy of the new millennium.

First, however, we turn to consider the role of sugar as big business. Global corporations are central players in the world sugar industry in all its facets: from production in the field and factory to consumption, and from trade on the commodity markets to influence in the renegotiation of trade agreements. In the next chapter we consider their role in the Caribbean. Have corporations reinforced the inequities generated by the role of sugar as a commodity? Do they play a part in the current crisis that the islands of the Caribbean face?

Chapter Three

Turning Cane into Cash:
Sugar as Big Business

'To do this job you've got to be hungry – you've got to really want to make money if you're going to thrive here. This is pressure.' (Trader on London Futures Market, 31 years old)

'If your children are hungry then you'll cut the canes. You've got to feed dem pickney' (Jamaican cane cutter, 42 years old)

Sitting behind a computer screen in an office in London, a young guy called Robert eats a Big Mac at his desk whilst watching the numbers flashing up on his computer screen. He's been at the office since seven this morning and is unlikely to leave before eight tonight. As he sips a Diet Coke, he answers the phone to his wife. They chat briefly about their youngest son and a problem with their nanny; he sends his love to his children as he says goodbye. He works such long hours that he doesn't see as much of his family as he would like, but thoughts of 'down-shifting' are still years away. His expenditure every month, just to run the house, is massive – a nanny, an au pair, the gardener. His eldest son has just got a place at one of the most esteemed fee-paying schools, and the second one will hopefully follow on soon. Unlike many of his colleagues, Robert himself failed to make it to Cambridge University and still feels a little insecure about his roots. But with the six figure salary he now earns and the half million pound bonus expected later this year, he's going to be able to make sure that his kids get all the advantages that he feels he missed out on.

Delroy has been in the cane field since five in the morning because he needs to finish cutting his canes before the sun gets too high in the sky. He's working alone because he can't afford the day rates this year for hired labour – he's had to divide the job over three days. It should be finished today and he'll be thankful – his back is so sore he couldn't sleep last night, and the blisters on his hands are weeping badly. As Delroy takes a break to eat the flour dumpling that his wife packed up for him, he thinks about the frustrations the year has brought him so far. There'd been the offer of a job conducting on a friend's bus, but it hadn't worked out. Then he'd missed out on getting work on the construction site for the new hotel that was going up in Montego Bay. Because they kept a good kitchen garden his family hadn't gone short of food yet; the thing that was really troubling him was his third son. The boy was bright and had earned a place at high school. But over the last few months there'd been no money and he hadn't been able to buy him new school shoes or books. Because of the shame of it his son had been missing out on a lot of attendance. This was the most troubling thing: more than anything Delroy wanted that boy of his to get a good start to make something of himself – to escape the cane cutting and the disappointments, and to be able to help the rest of them live an easier life.

Robert, at his desk in London, and Delroy, in his cane field in Jamaica do not, at first sight, appear to have a lot in common. Indeed, the circumstances of their lives could not be more different. But in fact there are a lot of similarities: they are both industrious individuals who work long hours; they are both devoted to their families; and they both want their children to benefit from opportunities that they never had. Moreover, in a much more obvious way their lives are actually closely connected. Through the work that they do, Robert and Delroy form links in a single chain of activity that connects the production of sugar to its consumption, and the cane field to the supermarket shelf. Through this chain, the labours of Delroy under the hot sun are linked to the fortunes of 'city slickers' in pin stripe suits; the payment of fees for the expensive education for Robert's child linked to the inability of Delroy to keep his boy in school. Robert may be able to retire at forty while Delroy will probably work until he dies; Robert will probably see his children achieve social and material success while Delroy may watch the talent of his son squandered through poverty. Both Delroy and Robert are moral individuals with laudable goals; neither has any understanding of the connection between them. For sugar is an enormous business that compartmentalises them into very separate cogs in the global productive wheel.

The inequalities between Delroy and Robert are the outcome of a multitude of factors, such as the inequality in trade and the impact of the commodity markets that was discussed in chapter two, and the local crisis in production described in chapter one. Big business links both of these. From the time in the nineteenth century when corporate interests began

*Cane cutter,
Guyana*

*Duncan
Simpson/
Panos
Pictures*

to replace family enterprise on the plantations in the Caribbean islands, productive interests concerned with the shipment, processing and distribution of cane sugar quickly merged. Over time these interests evolved into enormous companies which control each component of the chain.

Just as opinion is divided over the benefits or otherwise of special trade arrangements, so it is divided over the impact of the operations of these companies in vulnerable economies like Jamaica. As this chapter will explore, for some the view is that the activities of global corporations are neo-colonialist; for others, they are the modernising agents of job creation. Indeed, in the post-War period in the Caribbean this controversy has often been central to development planning; and, in contemporary times as we shall see, is critical too to the development dilemma which the Caribbean islands currently face. But inevitably, the role of big business in the production of sugar complicates even further the issues that were raised in the previous chapter, and further constrains opportunities for development.

65

This chapter considers the role of sugar as big business from three perspectives that link the disparate elements of production and consumption, and relate to the current crisis in the sugar economy of the Caribbean region. It begins with a broad overview of the role of multinationals in commodity production *per se* – exploring in general terms the relationship between business interests and the nature of the commodity trade. It then focuses specifically on the role of corporate capital in the industry in Jamaica. The financial markets – the stock exchange where sugar is bought and sold, and the futures market, where it is speculated – is the subject of the second part of the chapter. Through interviews with those involved in the negotiations of high finance on both sides of the Atlantic, the strange world of speculative trading through the computer screen is pieced together in the jigsaw of special trade arrangements and wider global governance.

At present, global corporations have penetrated the sugar industries of the different islands of the Caribbean to greater and lesser extents. Just as their nature of their trade arrangements varies between the islands, so does the nature of ownership of the industry itself.

In Jamaica, big business controls most of the plantations. While pockets of the old plantocracy survive in Barbados, ownership is largely mixed between state and private industry. In the Dominican Republic both state enterprises and sugar multinationals control the industry. The regional exception is Cuba, whose sugar-cane industry is entirely state owned, but even Cuba will eventually become enmeshed in sugar as big business on a global scale, through the futures market and the increasingly globalised nature of the trade. However, even the islands that trade all of their sugar through the Protocol still rely on corporations both for production and for brokering, as we will see.

Corporations and the commodity trade

According to *The Economist*, 500 corporations control 25% of the world's economic output. Indeed, the top 300 own 25% of the world's productive assets. Global corporate power has been steadily increasing for over 100 years, since the arrival of the limited stock company. Until the Second World War, expansion was very much structured through the nation state, under the system of liberal international capitalism. Since the 1950s, however – and led from the United States – corporations have continuously

Table 4
Sugar as a percentage of revenue of total
agricultural production

	Total agricultural production %	% of GDP	Ownership of sugar production
Barbados	41.4	1.8	mixed
Jamaica	13.9	1.0	state/private
St Kitts	74.0	28.0	state
Trinidad & Tobago	27.8	0.6	state

Source: ACP Group aide-memoire on ACP sugar, January 2000

increased in size, power and geographical range of influence. From the 1970s especially, the growth in corporate enterprise has been rapid: we now live in a world where the GDP of many of the poorer nation states is dwarfed by the annual turnover of the biggest global corporations. Moreover, the general trend, getting faster all the time, is towards ever increasing concentration – toward the control of markets and productive assets in the hands of fewer and fewer firms.

Global corporations often own the means of production, the transport facilities and the point of sale for the goods or services that constitute their business. Through vertical and horizontal integration they have come to control not just the factory floor where a car is made, for example, but the subsidiary companies that produce the component parts; not just the communications and media companies that produce advertisements, but also those that specialise in product design, or public relations. Often it is not even clear that a company is actually part of an 'umbrella' global corporation: a small 'independent' company with 50 employees may be bought by a corporation with a billion pound turnover world wide and 30,000 workers on their international books.

In the food commodity sector, corporate concentration is massive. As Tim Lang writes:

> At all levels – internationally, regionally, nationally, locally – a new baronial food class is emerging... The biggest three companies in world cocoa have 83% of the world market; the biggest three companies in tea have 85%; and so on. This process is accelerating. In 1989, the top 20 agrochemical companies had 94% of world markets; by the mid 1990s, the number with that market share was nearly halved.

The importance of huge corporations in the agricultural commodity sector has been obvious since the colonial era, when the great tea plantations in the East and the trade of the leaf itself became synonymous with the East India Company, while the West India Company controlled the shipment of sugar into Europe. In the consuming countries, Brooke Bond became a by-word for tea; Tate and Lyle for sugar and syrups. During the twentieth century Nescafé meant coffee to European consumers and Del Monte, the enormous tropical fruit producers, meant tinned pineapple and peaches. As these brands became associated with their products, the companies expanded their control upon the plantations where the raw goods were produced, the shipping and transport facilities that brought them to the West, and the processing plants that got them ready for the shop shelf.

In the world of sugar, for instance, Tate and Lyle, itself the result of amalgamation between two nineteenth century giants, merged part of its operations in the 1980s with another agribusiness giant, Booker. Both have interests in the sugar industries of Commonwealth countries. Today, Tate and Lyle and Booker both operate separately, but together operate a separate company known as Booker Tate, to improve their competitive position vis-à-vis other enormous agribusiness corporations.

Globalisation in practice

In the wider literature today there is continuing tension between the post war view of the global corporation as a *multinational*, and the observed evolution over recent decades of the *transnational*. A multinational corporation takes on many national identities, maintaining relatively autonomous production and sales facilities in individual countries, establishing local roots and presenting itself in each locality as a local citizen. Its globalised operations are linked to one another but are deeply integrated into the individual local economies in which they operate. The trend however, is toward *transnationalism*, which involves the integration of a firm's global operations around vertically integrated supplier networks.

Although a transnational corporation may choose to claim local citizenship when that posture suits it purpose, local commitments are temporary, and it actively attempts to eliminate considerations of nationality in its effort to maximise the economies that centralised global procurement makes possible. Key to this process is foreign direct investment (or FDI). Transnationals choose locations around the world where they decide to invest directly – this is not about trade with the said country, but about locating some part of global operations in a place that offers the best local conditions for the particular requirement. As David Korten has argued, in their day-to-day operations, the allegiance of the world's largest corporations is purely to their own bottom lines. However, for the purposes of seeking tax breaks, research subsidies, or governmental representation in negotiations that bear on their global marketing and investment interests, they 'wrap themselves in national flags and call for support from their 'home' governments'.

Globalisation is a multifaceted term that refers to cultural as well as economic processes. In relation to the latter, a simple definition might be the movement of industrial organisation from the local and the national, to the international. Contrary to the view of the media, globalisation is certainly not a new process – in fact it would probably be fair to say that it began with the voyages of discovery or even before. The nature of the modern world economy has developed over several centuries – indeed, as we explore in subsequent chapters, the wealth generated by the cane plantations of the Caribbean and the international trade of sugar had an important role in this. Globalisation, in its strongest formulation, however, is said to be a new stage of capitalism relating to the process described above – where global companies and financial institutions, attached to no particular nation state, move their capital around the world in search of the highest returns, and in so doing create a truly global market. Such global forces, it is argued, have severely limited the effectiveness of national government intervention.

As we will see, the process of globalisation is linked to the nature of international trade, and to the role of the global institutions that are meant to regulate the world economy, described in the previous chapter. Critically, the functioning of transnational corporations (TNCs) has an impact upon the current crisis in the Caribbean cane industry, both in terms of how it manifests itself at present and the development options that are available for the future. First, however, in order to understand more about their role, it is important to consider the historical benefits and costs that have been attributed to corporate penetration in commodity production in developing countries, and to consider how the different parts of the corporate jigsaw fit together.

For richer, for poorer: weighing up the costs

'The effects of TNCs on Third World economies are extraordinarily difficult to measure. In the continuing debate over their impact, Third World governments have usually given them warm support, while Non Governmental Organisations are often fiercely critical.... in no other area of development is there a bigger gap between governmental and NGO thinking than over the value or otherwise of these mammoth corporations.' John Madely, 1992

Just as corporations quickly emerged in the colonial period to consolidate their interests in the plantations of the Caribbean and Asia, the developing world today continues to hold many attractions for TNCs. Mining firms want to be located where minerals are to be found, and companies which produce consumer goods are attracted by the low rates of pay that prevail in most Third World economies, together with the frequent absence of organised labour unions. Developing countries remain an enormous source of agricultural commodities, with vast areas of the best land often devoted to cash crops for export even in food-deficit countries. Moreover, in the service sector, developing countries are becoming more and more important: as tourism grows year on year in 'exotic' territories, enormous foreign conglomerates often own the hotels that visitors stay in when travelling in developing countries.

Transnational corporations operate around the world, and regions of the North as well as the South are vulnerable to their activities. But in developing countries, this vulnerability is greatly intensified by the asymmetry of the relationship in terms of wealth and power. It is size that counts, and makes for an unequal relationship between government and corporation. Historically, in dealing with TNCs, the governments of developing economies have failed to get the best out of any investment deal, as the corporation holds most of the cards, in terms of the employment opportunities and other benefits that they offer. Moreover, TNCs are often heavily involved in the commodities or sectors that the developing economy itself is heavily reliant upon. Classically, poorer nations have undiversified economies that are often based around their colonial exports, such as sugar, groundnuts or rice; or rely very heavily on one or two extractive industries, such as bauxite extraction or petroleum; or have a very heavy dependence upon tourism. TNCs, therefore, are able to wield considerable power if their input is seen as central to these activities.

The nature of the internal operations of TNCs is also considered to have a negative impact upon developing countries. TNCs do not 'trade' in a true sense between different countries; rather, a sizeable proportion of the international trade conducted by them takes place actually within their own organisation. This may take place through a subsidiary in one country selling to and/or buying from a subsidiary in another, or exchanges may go through head office. By having subsidiary companies, TNCs are able to make use of a mechanism known as transfer pricing, which operates to the detriment of developing countries. As John Madely explains, under transfer pricing, the parent TNC sells materials to its subsidiaries in developing countries at artificially high prices. Such materials are then used in a manufacturing process or service industry. Having to pay these high prices reduces the profits of the subsidiary company, and means they pay less tax in the developing country where they operate – which is therefore cheated out of tax revenues. The difference between the declared profit of a TNC subsidiary and its real profit can be considerable.

Clearly, TNCs invest enormous amounts of money in developing economies, and on the surface, this seems welcome. But whether or not this investment results in a net gain is debatable. In fact, during the pre-debt decade of the 1970s, when Third World governments were striking out for self-determination, there was actually a period when they began to expropriate the assets of the huge corporations operating in their countries. Governments believed that by nationalising the operations run by TNCs, they could expropriate for their own countries the profits that were going to the corporations. In Jamaica, the sugar industry was nationalised under Michael Manley's government (described in detail in chapter five); the bauxite industry too became the target of attempted nationalisation, bringing Jamaica into direct conflict with the United States. This episode, however, was short-lived: by the end of the decade, Third World governments were reduced by debt into *de facto* receivership to the IMF and the auspices of structural adjustment.

It was also largely an unsuccessful period, leading to dramatic falls in the output and revenues of the targeted industries. TNCs are skilled at operating an economic activity at a profit – they would not stay in business otherwise. Governments quickly realised that they could not run the often quite complex, usually Western-style type of TNC operation with the same degree of profitability. The hoped-for gains from expropriation frequently failed to materialise, and nationalisation of TNCs was dropped as the answer to the problem; expropriation continues to be a largely abandoned approach.

Today, as a result of the lessons learned during the 1970s, the central tenets of structural adjustment programmes, and the basic lack of apparent alternative choices, developing economies generally welcome investment from TNCs. They are seen to be able to play a positive role in the industrialisation process in developing countries, because of their command over finance, technology and access to markets, and their capacity to plan, establish and manage complex organisations. They create jobs and therefore inject cash into the domestic economy, and they are seen to be engaged in a process of skill transference from developed to the developing world. But for the NGO sector and other commentators, there remain serious doubts over whether TNCs can really play a positive role in the trade and development efforts of poorer countries, unless they can be subject to more effective control – requiring global regulation at present simply not effected through the global institutions of governance. As David Korten writes:

> Less widely recognised is the tendency of corporations, as they grow in size and power, to develop their own institutional agendas aligned with imperatives inherent in their nature and structure that are not wholly under the control even of the people who own and manage them. These agendas centre on increasing their own profits and protecting themselves from the uncertainty of the market. They arise from a combination of market competition, the demands of financial markets, and efforts by individuals within them to advance their careers and increase their earnings. Members of the corporate

sector also tend to develop shared political and economic agendas. In the United States, for example, corporations have been engaged for more than 150 years in a process of restructuring the rules and institutions of governance to suit their interests.

Transnationals and the institutions of global governance

The previous chapter outlined how the nature of the international commodity trade has worked, since colonial times, to the disadvantage of developing economies. Commodity dependent countries have found themselves in a 'trade trap': unable, because of the nature of the 'world' market and the inequalities generated through special trade arrangements, to generate sufficient revenue to meet the basic needs of their home populations; yet so in need of foreign exchange to buy basic imports and service their debt obligations that they have no choice but to carry on devoting their resources into the production of the basic raw commodities that established this pattern of dependence in the first place. Today, as much as in the past, the workings of the world economy serve to perpetuate the weak position of the South.

The operation of multinational and transnational corporations appears to reinforce these circumstances. While corporations are not directly responsible for the nature of North/South trade they are, unlike the weaker producing countries, able to benefit from it. Moreover, their actions actively reproduce and maintain the status quo of the power relationship between the North and South. For a variety of reasons, in the world economy of today, global corporations have become a force for the continual reproduction of the system that locks regions like the Caribbean islands into crisis, rather than creating the potential for change.

To begin, as we have seen, the system of international trade has relegated developing economies into the position of the producers of basic commodities. The majority of the 'value added' refining or manufacturing of commodities is not undertaken in the country of origin, but rather, is transported to developed economies where that part of the manufacturing process which has the greatest value is undertaken. (Cane sugar, as we have seen is a good example in which the European Union does not allow refined sugar to be imported from the ACP nations. This arrangement has worked to the detriment of Jamaica, for example, but not to the detriment of Tate and Lyle, who have been able to control both the areas of production of cane sugar in the Caribbean needed for their own security of supplies, together with an enormous and profitable refining industry in Britain.) Moreover, in general, corporations need only choose to invest in those areas of commodity production where they are able to make a profit; unlike governments, they are not beholden to address the social concerns of job creation and community participation.

Global corporations are also able to benefit from the special trade arrangements that have been established between trading nations in an attempt to stabilise the conditions of trade for developing economies. In the Jamaican case again, Tate and Lyle and its sister companies have benefited from the ACP arrangements with the European Union that were described in the previous chapter. Tate and Lyle, like all of those engaged in the Jamaican sugar industry, receive the equivalent price for their sugar as that received by European beet farmers. Tate and Lyle provide the Jamaican government with a share of whatever profits they may accrue from operating the island's two largest estates, but unlike the government, they are able to limit their investment to the largest and most productive plantations on the island. This is not to say that no benefit has come to Jamaica through these arrangements, as the profitable operation of some of their sugar mills under the expertise of the company clearly has some positive repercussions. But, there is no doubt of the asymmetry of this relationship and, while the Jamaican industry as a whole languishes in crisis, Tate and Lyle as a whole continues to make good returns.

In a wider and more general sense, transnational corporations have also benefited from the debt crisis that has crippled the South over the last two decades, and the consequent structural adjustment programmes that have been the bankers' prerequisite for further lending. The global financial 'governance' institutions of the World Bank and the International Monetary Fund have overseen this process, while transnational companies have been central to its implementation.

As David Korten explains, in the 1970s, price increases imposed by the Organisation of Petroleum Exporting Countries (OPEC) placed oil-importing low-income countries in a critical foreign exchange position. At the same time, commercial banks were awash in petrodollars deposited by the OPEC countries and were looking for places to loan them profitably. There seemed to be an ideal fit between the needs of the banks and the needs of low-income countries. By this time, the World Bank's client countries had become accustomed to supplementing their export-based foreign exchange earnings with borrowing, and the line between foreign borrowing for self-liquidating investments and borrowing for current consumption had become badly blurred. Given the low real interest rates prevailing at the time that the OPEC money was being recycled through the system, the offers being made by the commercial banks seemed like a potential bonanza, and countries borrowed with abandon. Few on either side of the lending-borrowing frenzy seemed to notice that the whole scheme was a house of cards, dependent on borrowing ever more to cover debt service on former loans while still yielding net inflows.

Lending from the World Bank and its sister regional banks had been a fairly orderly process until the late 1970s, when the rise in oil prices effected by the OPEC countries caused the foreign debts of Southern countries to skyrocket. From 1970 to 1980, the long-term external debt of low-income countries increased from $21 billion to $110 billion; that of middle-income countries rose from $40 billion to $37 billion. As real interest rates soared, it became evident that the borrowing countries were so seriously overextended that default was imminent – leading potentially to a collapse of the whole global financial system. The World Bank and IMF, acting as overseers of the global financial system, stepped in – much as court-appointed receivers in bankruptcy cases – to set the terms of financial settlements between virtually bankrupt countries and the international financial systems.

In their capacity as international receivers, the World Bank and the IMF imposed packages of policy prescriptions on indebted nations under the rubric of structural adjustment, with two key underlying purposes. The first was to ensure that loans from both the commercial and the multilateral banks were repaid; thus, there was a strong emphasis on policies to strengthen exports and attract foreign investment in order to generate foreign exchange. Secondly, the aim was to advance the integration of domestic economies into the global economy. Import barriers were reduced or removed, based on the argument that this was necessary to improve access to materials used by export-orientated industries and to create competitive pressure to increase the efficiency of domestic firms so that they might, in turn, compete successfully in global markets.

As chapter two explained, the fact that dozens of countries have sought to increase their foreign exchange earnings by increasing the export of natural resources and agricultural commodities has driven down the prices of their export goods in international markets – creating pressures to extract and export even more to maintain foreign exchange earnings. Falling prices for export commodities, profit repatriation by foreign investors, and increased demand for manufactured imports stimulated by the reduction in tariff barriers have resulted in continuing trade deficits for most countries. From 1980, the beginning of the World Bank-IMF decade of structural adjustment, to 1992, low-income countries' excess of imports over exports increased from $6.5 billion to $34.7 billion. The Bank and IMF have responded with more loans as a reward for carrying out structural adjustment. David Korten argues that, rather than increasing their self-reliance, the world's low income countries continue to mortgage more of their futures to the international system each year.

However, structural adjustment has not hurt the global corporations. Whereas in the 1960s and 1970s they were facing mounting animosity in Third World countries, and even forced nationalisation, now they were being welcomed in to exploit the natural resources that their production operations needed, and to make profits in the most readily available areas. Whereas in the past there had been moves to enforce social obligation upon corporations around wage rates and employment opportunities, now governments were in no position of strength to argue such a case. In Jamaica, Tate and Lyle had left following bitter arguments with the Manley government over its insistence that the company would not be allowed to introduce mechanical harvesters and thus cut jobs; in the 1980s, they were humbly invited back to manage the two largest estates on the island. Again, David Korten sums up the relationship between the institutions of international regulation and the global corporations thus:

> Although it seeks to create an image of serving the poor and their borrowing governments, the World Bank is primarily a creature of the transnational financial system. The Bank's direct financial links to the transnational corporate sector on both the borrowing and the lending ends of its operation have received far too little attention. Technically, the Bank is owned by its member governments, which contribute its paid-in capital... although the Bank lends to governments, its projects normally involve large procurement contracts with transnational construction firms, large consulting firms, and procurement contractors. These firms are one of the Bank's most powerful political constituencies. The US Treasury Department is quite up front in its appeals to the corporate interest

in supporting funding replenishments for the Bank. For every one dollar the US contributes to the World Bank, more than two come back to US exporters in procurement contracts.

It is not just the World Bank and the IMF that have a close relationship with transnational corporations. The third institution in the Bretton Woods triumvirate – the General Agreement on Tariffs and Trade, now known as the World Trade Organisation – is also bound up with the world of corporate power. For critics like Korten, who see the World Bank and the IMF as having worked in concert to deepen the dependence of low-income countries on the global system, the GATT and its successor, the WTO, also appear to be open for use by the world's largest corporations to consolidate their power and place themselves beyond public accountability. Indeed, from some quarters, this third institution of global governance is held to be responsible for creating and enforcing a transnational corporate bill of rights.

Such a relationship clearly has wider implications for commodity producing countries throughout the South; but importantly, it relates to the crisis that the Caribbean islands currently face regarding the future of their special trade relationship with the European Union for their cane sugar. It is the World Trade Organisation, as we saw in chapter two, that has ruled such agreements as the banana protocol illegal and similarly targeted the Sugar Protocol; it is also under the auspices of the WTO that the EU has agreed to cut their support of European farmers (and thus the price paid to their Caribbean counterparts).

While these actions appear to be the result of protestations made by nation states, and especially the US, the corporate connection is strong. Although the WTO is an agreement among countries, and challenges are brought by one country against another, the impetus for a challenge normally comes from a transnational corporation that believes itself to be disadvantaged by a particular law. That corporation looks for a government that can be encouraged to bring a challenge. It need not be the government of its country of incorporation; a challenge can be brought by the government of any country that can make a reasonable case that its economic interest is being harmed.

However, the United States remains the dominant player in shaping international institutions such as the new WTO, and corporate interests have figured prominently in how the US has defined its national interest in relation to these and other global institutions.

Representatives of transnational corporations sit on US government and WTO committees; they spend millions of dollars on lobbying government; and thus, they have strong representation to the very organisation that sorts out disputes in international trade. According to Korten, the needs of the world's largest corporations are now represented by a global body with legislative and judicial powers that is committed to ensuring their rights against the intrusions of democratic governments and the people to whom those governments are accountable. And as we have seen over the last year, however, thousands of those people have taken to the streets in protest.

The development of this form of regulation in the private interest has been made possible because it has coincided with a political climate that sees the advance of 'free' markets as the advance of democracy. But markets are inherently biased in favour of people of wealth; even more important is that today they have a very strong bias in favour of very large corporations, which command far more massive financial resources than even the wealthiest of individuals. As markets become freer and more global, the power to govern increasingly passes from national governments to global corporations, and the interests of those corporations are free to diverge ever further from the kind of regulatory activity that we might hope for in the public interest. The Lomé Convention may benefit millions of poor people in the South, and even Tate and Lyle; but other transnationals with enormous investments in Central or Latin America want access to the EU for *their* produce, and will lobby to get that privilege.

In the last chapter, the Ricardian Theory of Comparative Advantage was advanced as the principle upon which international trade is said to work to the benefit of all participating countries. It is still regularly invoked as proof of the argument that free trade advances the public good. But when Ricardo originally articulated his premise in 1817, trade involved the exchange of finished national goods produced by national enterprises. Today, products are commonly assembled using components and services produced in many different countries. Global corporations, rather than national economies, are likely to be the co-ordinating units. Historically, those have obtained the benefits of this process held power in the global economy; as we move into the twenty-first century, transnationals as well as the countries of the North are those with this privilege. As such, their actions not only shape the current crisis for the Caribbean sugar industry, but also shape the limitations on future strategies for the production and trade of cane.

Corporations and sugar cane: the contemporary case of Jamaica

Chapters four and five explore the evolution and development of the sugar industries of the Caribbean, and the penetration of corporate enterprise into the islands' estates. Tate and Lyle, for instance, played an important role both in Jamaica and Trinidad from the 1930s onwards. In Jamaica, the activities of the company have been associated with some of the most significant episodes in the island's history: the social unrest that led to the formation of the country's political parties; the Great Sugar Debate when the country's intellectuals founded their own development agenda and urged the government to abandon the sugar industry altogether; the enormous upheavals of democratic socialism and the co-operative movement in the 70s; and debt and its consequences over the last two decades.

Following from their short-lived departure from Jamaica in the 1970s, Tate and Lyle has been a very important player in the activities of the industry for sixty years. Their arrival in the 1930s coincided with one of the lowest moments in the industry's history when sugar looked almost certain to collapse. But during the 1940s and 50s, spurred on by special trade arrangements with Britain, the industry grew greatly and Tate and Lyle's involvement could certainly be seen as having played a key role in the recovery. Today, their management capabilities and partial ownership of key parts of the industry are generally viewed by the government as critical to the industry's survival. Key Tate and Lyle personnel continue to play an advisory role to the Jamaican sugar industry as a whole, both in a local capacity, and as informants regarding the status of the current EU and WTO negotiations.

The controversy that courted the activities of Tate and Lyle in the island during the 1970s, however, has not gone entirely. The anti-colonial sentiments have dissipated, but sections of the Jamaican intelligentsia still view the company's manner of operation as having contributed to the current crisis at the local level. Tate and Lyle are accused of helping to maintain the lack of diversification in the rural economy, and of discouraging diversification within the industry because their global corporate needs are best met by encouraging inertia. Tate and Lyle are active in Jamaica because they want to guarantee their supply of raw cane sugar for their refineries in Europe, but they appear to have no interest in the production of alternative products from the sugar cane plant itself, or alternative uses of the land currently under cane. Just as the operations of global corporations maintain the status quo internationally between North and South, so Tate and Lyle stand accused of same thing at the local level, within the industry itself.

'The current situation today, in social terms and in economic terms, regarding the sugar industry, is bad... and when you look at it today you can sell a ton of sugar and you can barely buy 20 barrels of oil. Not only is the industry unable to pay its workers properly, but everything else is costing more... basically, the government themselves really have to be blamed because none of them really went out and looked at the different technologies that they could implement in the sugar industry...

And then there's Tate and Lyle. Tate and Lyle has its sugar factories, it has its refineries. It wants to get raw sugar to its refineries. That's it, so we have to stay in sugar... and we go along with it because we don't have a clear vision of what the alternative is. So we become captive of our own demise.

I would say that Tate and Lyle is doing nothing more than acting like the private sector – in their own best interests with their own bottom line. I think what they need to understand is that their bottom line can be protected without any great ill to them, but without the kinds of hardship that is on the people in developing countries, or the kinds of subsidies that the government has to put in it... because sooner or later people are going to get up and say, no we can't do this.'

Professor Al Binger, University of the West Indies

Giant transnational companies like Tate and Lyle dominate the world markets, moving goods from country to country by internal transfers, and fixing their own prices. Nevertheless there remains a further substantial element of the chain that links the production of sugar to its consumption. This gap is filled by the businesses that work as brokers or as traders, in and around the financial markets. This is the final component of sugar as big business.

We return now to the world that Robert, sipping his coke in front of his computer screen and concentrating his mind on the futures market, inhabits. The world from which Delroy, despite his best efforts, cannot benefit.

Managing risk in the commodity markets

In his book *Fair Trade: reform and realities in the international trading system,* Michael Barret Brown questions the role of a world market when production and distribution are in the same hands and controlled by companies operating on a global scale. In his words, producers have become traders; and traders, even big supermarket retailers like Sainsbury, have come to control production either directly or through sub-contractors. So then, what is the point of a market when production and distribution are in the same hands and controlled by companies operating on a global scale?

One answer is that there is still a part of world trade that does not go through the transnational companies, even if it is the lesser part. It may be that the big companies, which have not yet ceased to compete with each other, still need a market to set a price. The most obvious answer, however, is that they can make money out of markets by manipulation and speculation and at the same time manage the prices of exchanges that they do not control. As we saw in chapter two, sugar is the most volatile of all the commodities on the world market – it's price fluctuations over the last two decades have been severe. So a system has developed that allows the corporate world to deal with these uncertainties; but more than that, to profit from them.

Even with all the information available about markets and all the modern aids of market research, suppliers cannot know in advance what will sell well. This is particularly serious in the case of primary products, since it takes some time for production to be increased and cutting back entails costly waste of land and investment. It is partly the result of these uncertainties that giant transnational companies have become more and more involved in trading as well as in production.

Many of the commodity markets are based in London. For a long time they have provided the foundation of the City of London's wealth; indeed, through economic multiplier effects, everything from the state of the capital's property markets to the level of 'business confidence' are linked to their performance. There are also extensive commodity markets in New York and Tokyo and many narrower markets elsewhere such as Chicago and Singapore. But these markets are not like most markets where products are offered for sale and buyers choose according to taste and price.

There are several different kinds of principal players operating in the London commodity markets. *Physical* traders constitute the first type: they buy and sell commodities, keep them in stock if they expect prices to rise, and sell stock if they expect them to fall. Both buyers and sellers represent the very big companies, but the sellers are generally selling the products of many producers, even millions, while the buyers are generally buying for one of two powerful companies. By playing the market the big companies can insure themselves against sudden changes in price. By far the largest number of operators in the commodity markets, however, are not really trading in commodities at all but in *futures* – in paper titles to commodities.

Trading on the future

Futures trading actually evolved in London in the eighteenth century, from the public auctioning of imported goods. This was a time of great voyages of international trade setting out from the Thames to fetch sugar, tea, coffee and cocoa, amongst other things. As Belinda Coote explains, the mere buying and selling of these goods did not provide the shippers, in particular, with insurance for their cargoes. Their ships had to undergo long and hazardous voyages to get the goods from Asia or Latin America to the City of London; they therefore needed some guarantee that they would be able to cover their costs and pay their crews, and so the practice of buying and selling in the future began. To do this, merchants in the City of London had to take views on what the forward price of a shipment of, for example, copper would be in three months time – its expected date of arrival from Santiago. They would do this by assessing the likelihood of its arrival, on time or at all, and the projected demand for it.

Today, futures trading remains based around the same principle. In the balancing of demand and supply, the expectations of supplies available or expected to be available at future dates are set against the demands placed for supplies now and in the future. As a result of the interest charged for borrowing money or the interest on capital forgone in purchasing and storing commodities, there are, depending on the rate of interest ruling at any time, different prices for any product – a price (the spot price) for delivery today, a price for delivery in one month, three months, six months and even longer (futures or forward prices).

Any two parties can agree to a price for forward delivery i.e. delivery in a few weeks or months. Futures prices, however, are the result of the influence of a whole range of dealers outside the markets who are in effect speculating on changes in the prices of commodities. Depending on whether there are shortages or surpluses at the time or expected in the future, prices can rise and fall not just by a few percentage points but in great booms and slumps. There are fortunes to be made out of gambling on these changes. In part, the speculative element arises from the desire of dealers and their customers to insure against violent changes. The dealer who is hedging is bearing the risk, but if s/he is successful he will be taking a profit, sometimes a very large one. So, the main reason for speculation is the money that is to be made out of it, on top of the market price of the commodity.

The final complicating factor is that because of the money to be made from speculating in commodities, by far the largest number of commodity traders are not physical traders; they know absolutely nothing about the commodities or future trends in demand and supply. They are called *technical* traders. Commodity speculation is a risky business like any other form of gambling and requires a fair amount of money to start with. The technical dealers employ 'systems' on the basis of which they buy or sell different commodities. The systems are constructed on past and current movements or prices extrapolated into the future. These are built on computer programmes and, as new information is fed in, the computer signals whether and when to buy or sell a particular commodity. These instructions are then passed to brokers on the floor of the exchanges.

The scale of futures trading, having evolved several centuries ago, has actually rocketed in the last two decades. The increasing activity in the markets today of the technical dealers has meant that the prices that emerge are only in part the result of any kind of rational estimate of future trends. By hedging and other operations the dealers may take some of the risk out of the business on behalf of the buyers and producers, although as we have seen the dealers are often big producers themselves. But far from having a smoothing effect as it is sometimes claimed, the futures market can easily exaggerate the up and down swings. It is the growers, especially the small growers, who suffer most from these swings, gaining little from the upswings and often losing heavily on the downswings.

To trade in futures requires capital. To hold a margin account you have to be credit-worthy, and the sums of money involved are great. As a result, it is large companies who benefit from the transactions and control the marketplace. Just as the role of corporate capital *can* be of great benefit to developing economies, so futures trading *can* be a simple and effective way of stabilising producer prices. Yet the prohibitive sums of money involved exclude the involvement of the people who most need stable prices. Few developing countries trade in futures. Their contracts may be too short for them; and they lack the necessary credit. It is not the principles of the market that are at fault. If those same principles could be applied on a small scale, millions of producers in developing countries in theory would benefit from the reduction in the unpredictability of their incomes.

Joining up with Robert and Delroy

Just like Delroy, the world of work that Robert inhabits has its own traditions and habits – working principles that shape routine and specialised language that means little to those not involved. Just like work in the cane fields, work patterns on the futures markets do not fit in around a nine to five schedule – it is done in shifts, with people coming in to the office at ten in the morning to work till late evening, or in the early hours to stay until late afternoon. In Gaythorne, even young children understand the routines of the harvest and the crop cycle; similarly, on the futures market, everyone can share in the common language of *long of it, short of it, bullish, bearish, buy and sell*. (If you're long of it you've already bought, you own something or you're growing it.) But whereas in Jamaica, young people will go to enormous lengths to avoid working in the sugar industry, in London, young people will go to great lengths to try to secure a job as a trader. For them, working in this part of the sugar business offers the potential of enormous financial returns, and the comforts of a high-earning urban lifestyle.

As mentioned above, not all of the sugar that is traded internationally goes through the futures market. Indeed, because Jamaica receives a guaranteed price for its sugar, it has no need to trade on the future at all. (The sugar of other Caribbean islands, however, is variously traded through

Technical checks on sugar production, Guyana   Duncan Simpson/Panos Pictures

special trade arrangements *and* the world market, and therefore, will be, traded via the futures market to a varying extent.) Because of its relationship with Tate and Lyle, however, Jamaica does need to employ the services of a 'middleman'.

The arrangement that there is between Tate and Lyle and Jamaica is set out in a long-term contract, according to a price reflecting the protocol price. The EU regulation which sets out the overall package of controls and limitations is incorporated in the commercial contract. Tate and Lyle has a commercial contract with the producers, and the producer employs a broker to act as its representative in its relationship with Tate and Lyle. The broker is responsible for overseeing a collection of contractual obligations: the administration, the timing, the documentation and the payment, and even the insurance or chartering. Any problems arising also go through the broker, to avoid confrontation with the buyer.

We now turn to the London-based company that operates both as a futures trader on the sugar market *per se*, and as a broker for Jamaica. Here, a senior trader describes the day-to-day running of the office and the range of activities that take place. It is a busy, open plan environment, with rows of youthful looking men, and the occasional woman, sitting in front of computer screens. At the desks along one wall, they're trading sugar; the following row is trading coffee, and the one in front of that is trading cocoa.

'There isn't an instant way to becoming a senior trader. They come from all walks of life... you've got the absolute East End trader that used to be known as a barrow boy, and you've got the high flying merchant bank graduate – and both elements you need to make that financial futures element work... You get a nose for when to buy and sell and how to transact. You need an aggressive street-wise attitude.

There is a way of deciding price movement by what's called technical analysis, where you look at the movements on charts, and it's almost a science. By looking at what a market has done in the past, it will give you a prediction for the future... Some prefer that sort of analysis. They're not interested in the fact that there's a drought in Africa and the crop is expected to be down. They're interested just in price, which is where a great deal of the speculative element of the market is going from and then you start with this enormous fund trading.

With futures, for someone who has been used to buying an investment and selling it when it's gone up in value, it's a very difficult concept to grab, that you can actually sell something that you haven't got and buy it back again and again before you receive it as if you've never had it in the first place. A ton of sugar produced from anywhere in the world can be traded across the exchanges of the world twenty times the actual tonnage amount before that sugar is even shipped. So if you take 50 tons of sugar, the contracts to the equivalent of 20 times that – i.e. a thousand tons, will have been traded across the world's exchanges. And it's probably more than that. Sometimes even before that sugar is grown, let alone shipped.

On the futures markets, there are people who are purely trading on pieces of paper, never ever trade the physical commodity. In fact that is probably the bulk of them these days. So they are speculators, they are investment people, they are funds. And funds now could be three billion dollars to invest. Enormous money moves markets. The people trading the pieces of paper frequently never have an interest in the physical commodity; they are only interested in the fact that the sugar price could go up and down, and they are trying to work out which way and trade it correctly.

But then there is the actual physical trade, if you like, the genuine business behind it. Where a producer country knows its going to produce a certain amount of sugar, but by the time its grown and they're ready to ship it, the world price will have moved. It's better for them to hedge, and by that I mean sell a paper contract that would lock in a price level while they're still finishing the end of their growing season. It's no good them investing in a cane field growing it, irrigating it, fertilising it, cutting it and getting it to port, only to find the world price has dropped below their cost of production. They'll have a price in mind that they are happy to accept, and they will sell some people contracts to lock that in. That's the producer.

The consumer has also got to consider his risk. He knows he's going to need to import sugar, sometime over the next six months. The timing of that could be down to a whole host of reasons. If he waits to the last minute, till he's ready to import, again, the price could be very right or very wrong. So he will buy pieces of paper, because until he's actually imported it, he's going to be short of the commodity he knows he's going to need. So he needs to cover that short by buying pieces of paper.

If I'm a producing country and I have a crop disaster, and I don't produce the sugar that I thought I was going to and the rest of the world thought I was going to, surely the world price will go up? In which case, I have sold a piece of paper contract, the world price is going up, and if I've got to buy back my piece of paper, it's going to cost me more to buy it back. And you'd be absolutely correct. The timing is, to realise that your crop is a disaster and buy the piece of paper before anyone else knows, and the price has gone up. And that's the game.

One of our main activities here is to act as a broker to the ACP countries. Covering Barbados, Jamaica, Guyana, Belize, St Kitts. Now of all the ACP sugar that has the quota into Europe, 1.3 million tons of sugar comes to Tate and Lyle, to their refineries. It comes from 16 sugar producing ACP members. The ACP producer, on the Sugar Protocol, the futures market is not good to him. Because he is getting a fixed price from the EU which is roughly three times the world price. So you can not hedge something three times higher than the world market... when the agreement was made, all the sugar was then coming to Tate and Lyle. It isn't just the price, you've then got to agree shipping schedules. Freight, the producer, has to pay for getting the sugar to Tate and Lyle. You have to make sure of the correct documentation, any delays... finance.

These companies are almost trading with themselves. They have expanded so that they have interests in the producing countries. The large sugar groups have the expertise, so I think countries decided, well, if we're going to refine some here, or open a new processing there, we may as well use the expertise of certain trusted companies... they can at least produce a decent crop and run an efficient refinery.'

Multinationals such as Tate and Lyle assist in the maintenance of the status quo at the local level, contributing to the lack of diversification within the rural economies of the Caribbean islands where they operate. For all that they arguably contribute, global corporations are fair weather friends to developing economies. As the Lomé Convention is rescinded, and the Protocol price reduced, the operations of Tate and Lyle are unlikely to maintained in the fading sugar industries of the Caribbean.

Big business, small benefit

Sugar as big business complicates further the development problems that the commodity markets have presented to the Caribbean. At the local level, for instance, Tate and Lyle appears to have acted as a force of stagnation rather than development. At the global scale, moreover, transnational companies in general have contributed to the circumstances of international governance that now threaten the very existence of the region's sugar industry. Of course, the picture is a complicated one, and the effects of TNCs on the Third World in general are extremely difficult to measure. But while the investment, wealth and job creation that these corporations are capable of must hold potential for the Caribbean, until the present they appear to have done little to contribute towards diversification and development within the sugar industry – as the circumstances of the lives of those working in the cane fields testify.

As we will see, the apparent willingness of government to accept the status quo has not always been there. History, however, has taught the Caribbean some harsh lessons regarding its ability to confront the powerful players on the international stage. The following two chapters explore the history of the Caribbean region through the window of the sugar industry, from its establishment until present. What is the historical context of the current crisis? What opportunities now present themselves for the future?

Chapter Four

Sugar and Strife: Europe and the Evolution of the Caribbean Sugar Industry

'Splendour, dress, show, equipage, everything that can create an opinion of their importance, is exerted to the utmost of their credit. They are thought rich; and they are so indeed, at the expense of the poor Negroes who cultivate their lands... an opulent West Indian vies in glare with a nobleman of the first distinction.' (Description of absentee planter in London, 1765)

Although sugar was known in England and in Europe as early as the twelfth century, it remained for centuries a rare and precious product, used only by a few for medicinal and condimental purposes. By the seventeenth century the wealthy of England were able to consume it frequently; by the nineteenth century it was a major source both of energy, and solace, to the British working classes. As Sidney Mintz in his 1985 classic text, *Sweetness and Power*, has written, the development of the 'sweet tooth' for which the British are renowned was entirely dependent upon the establishment of sugar production in the islands of the Caribbean. It was from this beginning that sugar became a ubiquitous foodstuff and an agricultural commodity produced, traded and consumed globally. The patterns of commodity trade that have been described evolved from the initial colonisation of the Caribbean region – where, for more than three centuries, sugar was King and Europe was Governor General.

While sugar made an important contribution to the palatability of the European diet, its value to the economic development of its colonisers was immeasurable. The Caribbean sugar plantations were of huge importance to the metropolitan economies of the seventeenth, eighteenth and nineteenth centuries, because of the wealth that sugar generated for them and the markets that the islands themselves provided for European goods. Indeed, in both an economic and social sense, the history of the sugar islands of the Caribbean has been intimately connected with that of European development. It was in the Caribbean that the wars between the Spanish, French, British and Dutch were fought in the battle for colonial supremacy; it was through the marketing of sugar that they developed new forms of economic behaviour and international trade. Moreover, it was even the same momentum that eventually created a world economy. And, as we will see, the origins of the crisis that presently paralyses the Caribbean sugar industry lie in this colonial period, when the fortunes of the islands became enmeshed with the economic imperatives of the West.

Although the wealth extracted from the Caribbean became the catalyst for change in Europe, the impact upon the islands themselves of European settlement and colonisation was profound and complete. The Caribbean region is unique, in fact, in that it is entirely post-colonial. Over the course of three centuries, under the jurisdiction of Europe, its economic and social structure was completely conditioned by sugar production. Under the abomination of slavery new societies were born, and through the confines of plantation agriculture, new economies were shaped. As this chapter will explain, the timing of events under the different European powers created variation in the circumstances in each particular island, and physical geography conditioned the extent to which each was dominated by cane production. But across the region as a whole, history has left the indelible imprint of sugar-cane production. Understanding this history is key to understanding the dilemma of plantation production with which the contemporary Caribbean continues to wrestle.

Establishment of sugar-cane production: the sixteenth and seventeenth centuries

By the early decades of the seventeenth century when the British, Dutch and French established colonies in the Caribbean, the first epoch of the region's encounter with sugar-cane production was already over. During the fifteenth century, Portugal and Spain had experimented with sugar cane and from here it had been carried to the New World by Columbus on his second voyage in 1493. During the Spanish conquest sugar production was established throughout the islands of the Greater Antilles, spreading during the sixteenth century from Hispaniola to Jamaica, Puerto Rico and Cuba.

The Spaniards' aim in coming to the Caribbean had been the three 'G's: to gain Glory and Gold and to serve God. Claiming possession of

The Spaniards on Hispaniola force slaves to cultivate sugar   Theodor de Brys/Mary Evans Picture Library

many of the islands, and the mainland of Central America, on behalf of the King and Queen of Spain, they had been looking both for riches and for heathens to convert to the Christian religion.

Sugar grown in Hispaniola was first shipped back to Europe as early as 1516. The Spaniards, however, were more interested in searching for wealth more easily acquired than through settlement agriculture, and turned their attention to Mexico and Peru in the search for gold. For more than two centuries afterwards, Spain's emphasis remained on the mainland, and its Caribbean possessions served primarily as way stations and fortresses along trade routes. But as sugar production dwindled in the Spanish Caribbean, a burgeoning sugar industry was established by the Portuguese in Brazil, and the sixteenth century became the Brazilian century for sugar. Meanwhile, within the Spanish New World, the early achievements in Hispaniola and the rest of the Caribbean had been outstripped by developments on the mainland, where sugar cane prospered in Mexico, Paraguay and the Pacific coast of South America.

This was a period of religious zealotry and intense economic rivalry between European nations. It was also a time of exploration, and inevitably European squabbles made waves in the Caribbean Ocean. The Spanish government had to face the almost continuous efforts of other Europeans to break into its empire. The Portuguese, with their common devotion to the Catholic Church, co-operated with the Spanish; but the French, English and Dutch wanted their share of the overseas booty and the English, especially, were successful at getting it. During the seventeenth century, with the help of such Elizabethan notables as Francis Drake and Walter Raleigh, England fought the most wars, conquered the most colonies, and began an irreversible process of territorial expansion. Although during the seventeenth century both the French and the Dutch established colonies in the Caribbean, the English settler population far exceeded that of either of her two principal north European rivals.

The islands of St. Kitts and Barbados were settled first as permanent crop-growing colonies and both the English and the French experimented to find a satisfactory commercial crop. The first experiment was with tobacco but this faced stiff competition from Virginia; various attempts were also made to cultivate cotton and indigo. Then in the 1640s, as the demand for sugar increased at home, the English began to grow sugar cane in Barbados. From this origin, sugar was to crystallise the formation of new Caribbean societies. The British sugar industry expanded rapidly, engulfing Barbados and soon after Jamaica and driving Portuguese sugar out of the north European trade. By 1655, Barbados had no serious competitors in sugar production and was the richest English territory in the Americas.

The early plantation system

The system of sugar production itself that was established during the latter half of the seventeenth century also set a precedent, for it changed relatively little as it was subsequently spread from island to island. The system had an *internal* and *external* structure, the first defining how sugar cane was produced on the island itself and the latter, its relationship with Europe. Over the course of time new laws were passed by England and France which influenced the manner in which they governed their colonies, but they served only their basic intention of maximising the wealth of the colonial powers.

The method of cane production which constituted the *internal* structure was borrowed from Brazil: the technology of water and animal-powered sugar mills, and the processes for grinding, boiling and manufacturing sugars and molasses from the extracted juice, as well as for distilling rum from molasses. The design of the plantation buildings necessary for the efficient running of the sugar estates – the plantation house where the owner lived, the mill complex and the huts for the labour force – were also borrowed from the Brazilians. As Henry Hobhouse describes in *Seeds of Change:*

> The canes were crushed in mills and the sugar then boiled out of the cane in a series of open vats in a sugar house... In the seventeenth century a small, primitive, on-farm mill would only produce molasses and one grade of sugar. The heat was fierce, since there was no means of cooling the sugar house. Temperatures of 140 degrees Fahrenheit were recorded... Humidity would also be very high and therefore exhausting. It was a job for... slaves, not free men.'

Indeed, from the very beginning the fledgling Barbadian sugar plantations used slave labour, in the same fashion as the Portuguese, from Africa. This was not the region's first introduction to slavery; nor, during the early years of Barbados settlement was it the most dominant form of labour. But the establishment, in the seventeenth century, of a relationship between Caribbean sugar production and African slave labour was set to determine one of the most extreme and globally significant human traumas in history. So enormous was its impact that it is almost impossible to summarise; but suffice to say that it was to lead to the creation of entirely new societies throughout the region, where race, social hierarchy and sugar production would become intimately connected.

The first epoch of the Caribbean sugar experience in the sixteenth century had involved the forced labour of both the indigenous Indians and Africans. The Portuguese were already enslaving Africans from the Guinea coast when the Spanish first settled in Hispaniola, and from 1505 onwards the Spanish government began sending some of these people to the New World. Mortality amongst them was extremely high; however, unlike the decimated local Indian population, they were replaceable and so the trickle of slaves across the Atlantic grew stronger. This early Caribbean slave trade collapsed with the Spanish sugar industry. By the

Slaves in a sugar mill, Jamaica, early 1800s   *Illustrated London News, Mary Evans Picture Library*

time of its resurrection in the seventeenth century, however, the association between dark skin and slave labour had already been established. While white *indentured* labour was still being used, it was insufficient for the demands of sugar cultivation and African slavery quickly became crucial to the success of the early plantations. In 1645, Barbados had about 5,500 African slaves; by 1667, it has been estimated that it had more than 80,000.

Eric Williams, in the classic *From Columbus to Castro*, relates to the picture provided by the English historian, Sir Thomas Dolby, of the sugar industry at the end of the seventeenth century:

> The typical sugar plantation comprised about one hundred acres, forty of which were planted to cane, forty allowed to lie fallow, and twenty used for pasture, provisions, and as a nursery for canes. The plantation was equipped with a windmill, which turned the great iron rollers, and it had a boiling house, still-house, curing-house, drying house and other buildings for manufacturing the sugar. The labour force amounted to fifty Negro slaves, seven white servants, together with an overseer, a doctor, a farrier and a carter. The plantation had six horses and eight oxen. Land, buildings, slaves, servants and livestock together represented a capital investment of £5 625 sterling. The plantation produced annually 80,000 pounds of sugar – that is, fewer than its gigantic twentieth century counterpart produces – about 35 tons, or less than one ton per

acre, and twenty hogsheads of 700 pounds each of molasses. After deducting expenses for clothing, wear and tear of tools, and necessary supplies, the sugar and molasses, sold in the West Indies, yielded £540, or an annual profit of nearly ten per cent.

The nature of the actual trade of slaves quickly became central to the *external* structure of the early plantation system. During the first years of sugar cultivation in Barbados, the planters had bought their slaves from the Dutch. The slave trade generated great wealth, however, and in 1660 the Navigation Act was passed in England which made sure that English planters bought their slaves from English merchants instead. In return, they received a virtual monopoly of the British national sugar market. Similar legislation was also passed by the French government regarding their Caribbean colonies. This arrangement, known as *mercantilism,* ensured that all the wealth extracted from the islands remained in the hands of the colonial powers.

Mercantilism preceded the theory of comparative advantage that chapter two described; as the first rationale for international trade, it held that 'demand' was a constant for any people or country, and that overall profit from trade could not be increased – each nation, therefore, must try to get the greatest share for themselves. This meant that the colonies must buy and sell from the 'motherland' only, and cargoes must be transported across the Atlantic only in her ships. The imposition of mercantilism upon the islands not only cemented the nature of the external structure of the plantation system and the relationship between the islands and Europe; it was also the very first step toward the position of dependency that the contemporary Caribbean islands occupy today in the world sugar economy.

During the final years of the seventeenth century commodity trade increased, and the commercial status of the West Indian colonies was steadily enhanced. The principles of mercantilism were even more deeply entrenched when the King of England granted the Royal Africa Company a monopoly in respect of the slave trade, and legislated for two further Acts which required that goods supplied from one colony to another should be liable to English import tax. And in addition to the protected sugar market in England, the colonies also, in return, got naval support in the Caribbean. This, however, was just a sweetener for what was to come.

The Barbadian chapter of the Caribbean sugar story drew to a close with the end of the seventeenth century. As land fertility declined and the circumstances of trade changed, profits fell, and the focus of production passed to Jamaica. This early experience however, set an important trend: throughout its subsequent history, sugar-cane production has bloomed and wilted in succession in different English, French and Spanish Caribbean islands. After being brought into the sphere of European influence when plantation agriculture was established, each has remained in production; but the early 'boom' periods that were variously experienced by different islands in the seventeenth, eighteenth and nineteenth centuries have left permanent legacies of decay.

Sugar in the eighteenth century Caribbean: the rise of Jamaica

If sugar was King in the eighteenth century Caribbean, then Jamaica was the jewel in his crown. As the focus of Caribbean sugar production switched from Barbados, sugar cane swept across the fertile lowlands of Jamaica as English planters took their chances with one of the world economy's first commodities. Not all of them succeeded, for even during the 'boom' periods of the eighteenth century, sugar production was beset with the risks of crop failure, hurricanes and drought, and trade was often hindered by the European wars fought out in the Caribbean Sea. Indeed, for some of the most daring entrepreneurs, their reward was to end their days in debtors' prison. But for others, sugar turned to gold in the Caribbean sunshine and they became very, very rich indeed.

As the eighteenth century progressed, sugar production spread to almost every parish in Jamaica and the island became the centre of the West Indies sugar trade. At its peak, it was the largest sugar exporter in the world, with the parish of Trelawny, as described in chapter one, at the centre of the island's industry. This achievement produced a society – an internal plantation structure – that was geared entirely towards sugar production and stratified according to the hierarchy of the plantation. British plantation owners and managers stood at the pinnacle of society, with African slaves at the lowest level of the social order.

Social stratification amongst the slaves was according to their division of labour on the plantation: those slaves who worked in the planter's house as domestics were of higher status than the skilled slaves who worked in

Cutting cane, Antigua, 1833   *The Saturday Magazine, Mary Evans Picture Library*

the sugar mills, and who in turn were ranked higher than the fieldworkers who were chained together in gangs to weed and cut the cane. These divisions between the slaves were also based on the correlation of colour and status. Over time, a mixed race or mulatto group developed and occupied a middle caste position between the whites and the slaves, and within the slave group itself, the less menial tasks were performed by those of mixed race.

For the slaves, the plantation was an inhumane, pervasive institution that dominated, reculturised and inflicted indescribable cruelty. The planters deliberately sought to mix up the different tribes to suppress African languages and prevent the slaves communicating with each other. All cultural symbols and relations of African origin were suppressed too. Under the whiplash of the drivers, they were often worked to death. Indeed, many planters thought it more economic to do so and buy more slaves, rather than to lessen the workload and spend more on food so that they would live longer. Over the years, many slaves pre-empted this fate and chose suicide, when all other options of escape were denied them. As Hobhouse notes:

> Sugar, then, is the most notable addiction in history that killed not the consumer but the producer. Every ton represented a life. Every teaspoonful represented six days of a slave's life.

98

In so far as output was concerned, the eighteenth-century sugar plantation was still a dwarf. According to Williams, in 1768 Jamaica had 648 plantations, of which 369 were equipped with cattle mills, 235 with water mills, and 44 with windmills. The total production was 68,160 hogsheads, or a little over 100 hogsheads (80 tons) per mill. The number of slaves required to produce one hogshead of sugar varied from 1 to 2.5; the island average was 1.66, or about two slaves to every ton of sugar. Not a single innovation had been made either in technology or cultivation as compared with the preceding century. The eighteenth century plantation was a version differing only in date from the story begun in Hispaniola in the sixteenth century and continued in Barbados in the seventeenth. Contemporaries estimated that less than one-third of the Jamaican industry was efficient, and that one-seventh of a crop was regularly wasted by neglect and want of foresight.

Meanwhile, up at the Great House, as the planters' increasingly elaborate plantation houses came to be known, a life of rum-soaked decadence ensued for the plantocracy – or at least, those who decided to reside in Jamaica. A spoilt, uneducated and increasingly inbred expatriate crowd, they talked apparently only of the price of sugar, the damage done by the latest hurricane and the 'wickedness' of the slaves, as they were waited on by their servants and feasted at every meal. As Williams recounts:

> From twenty to forty domestic servants were not unusual in a single household. The list in one household includes: one butler; two footmen; one coachman; one postillion; one helper; one cook; one assistant; one storekeeper; one waiting maid; three house cleaners; three washerwomen; four seamstresses. Each child in the family had to have its nurse, and each nurse her assistant boy or girl.

The Jamaican social structure was also influenced by the high rates of absenteeism amongst the planter class that were typical of all the plantation islands in the Caribbean at the time. As the English planters left for the mother country, the original Scottish and Irish servants, and their descendants, came to dominate the senior positions of the Jamaican community. Thus Jamaica had a dual elite system: one, an absentee elite, predominantly English; and the other, the resident plantocratic elite which was predominantly Celtic in origin.

In England, the absentees became influential figures like the famous William Beckford. As the grandson of the planter Peter Beckford, who had himself been reputed to be the richest man in Europe at the time of his death, William lived in ostentatious style symbolised by his imposing Wiltshire country seat, Fonthill Splendens. William and his brothers, like other absentees, bought seats in Parliament and together constituted the most powerful political lobby of the century, known as the West Indian Interest. While in Parliament they lobbied to secure continued protected markets for their sugar in Britain; outside of it, they indulged themselves in their wealth.

Back in Jamaica, meanwhile, as the planters imported that which they consumed and exported that which the mother country desired, the seeds for long-term economic dependency were being sown. Firstly, there was no effort made to establish the basis of civil society: there was little investment in education as children were generally sent to school in England, and the island was destitute of any kind of social services or administration.

Secondly, and even more seriously, no thought was given to the establishment of an indigenous agriculture. The main activities on the estate revolved around sugar cane and, with the exception of the 'provision grounds' which the slaves were given on which to grow their own food, there was no serious attempt made for self-sufficiency. Then, as now, sugar production itself involved only a small number of processes – growing and harvesting the cane, grinding it to extract juice and boiling it to a syrup – to produce brown unrefined sugar. The refining process into fine white sugar was done in England.

This division in the production process was the third major root of future economic handicap. From the outset, colonial legislation was established to tax refined sugar heavily and thus strangle at birth an island refining industry – a policy that was pursued throughout the Caribbean and which has been to the permanent detriment of the region. As their economies were geared, for the indefinite future, towards export agriculture, the islands of the region were unable to harness for themselves that part of the production process with the greatest potential for 'value-added' linkages and indigenous economic growth. The subservient role of Jamaica, and the other islands in the region, was firmly reinforced as the international economy emerged.

Only the activity of the slaves on their provision grounds went some small way to mitigate against this trend of external dependency. The slaves were given some time – generally Sunday – to cultivate their own food;

William Beckford's Fonthill Abbey, Wiltshire, 1822   *Engraving, J Barnett/Mary Evans Picture Library*

quickly, the surpluses that they generated were being traded in Jamaica at Sunday markets. As Sidney Mintz describes in *From Plantations to Peasantries in the Caribbean*:

> Long before the end of the period of apprenticeship (1838), Jamaican slaves were producing not only most of their own subsistence but also an astoundingly large surplus of foods, the bigger part of which ended upon the tables of free people, including the planters themselves. In effect, what had begun as a technique for saving the planters the costs of supplying their slaves with food had then become an essential basis for the food supply of the non-slave population. Were it not such a deplorable comment on slavery itself, it would be funny to realise that the British garrisons maintained in Jamaica before emancipation 'to keep order' were almost entirely provisioned by the slaves, working on their own time. One writer, an enthusiastic supporter of slavery at that, concluded that perhaps as much as 20 per cent of the metallic currency in Jamaica at the end of the eighteenth century was in the hands of the slaves. Not only had the production of foodstuffs on plantation land allocated to slaves become a major feature of Jamaican life, but the free population was also now dependent upon it – and this in a society

101

where, to all intents and purposes, there were no free agricultural workers of any kind... on the one day a week that slaves were grudgingly given for themselves, their behaviour on their little garden plots completed contradicted the planters' insistent claims that 'stupid, lazy savages' were incapable of working intelligently for themselves. These, then, were the proto-peasants: enslaved Africans and their descendants... under the lash, yet asserting their own essential humanity, initiative, and intelligence, in the face of every cruel limitation.

As the eighteenth century progressed in Jamaica, and sugar production expanded, the planter-class became increasingly anxious about the manageability of their enterprises and their own personal safety – an anxiety that increased with time as the number of slaves necessary to labour on the expanding sugar estates increased. As more and more slaves were imported, and the ratio of white people to black people fell, the development of the Jamaican sugar economy advanced the ethnological transformation which had begun in Hispaniola in the sixteenth century and continued in Barbados in the seventeenth.

According to Williams, in 1698 there was one white for every six blacks in Jamaica. By 1778, the whites numbered 18,420 and the slaves 205,261 – a ratio of eleven blacks to one white. The plantocracy lived in perpetual fear of slave rebellion and indeed had good reason to, as over the course of the century there were a dozen serious revolts by the slaves. Greed however, sustained them, and as their wealth increased in line with the acreage of their sugar cane, they flagrantly breached the laws that limited the proportions of black to white on the island's sugar plantations.

Sugar and economic change in England

It was not only the planters who got rich. The infamous triangle that connected Jamaica, England and Africa brought great wealth to England (as did the triangle that connected France with Africa and the French colonies). In fact, some commentators have suggested that the wealth extracted from slavery and sugar spurred on England's industrial revolution and the movement from mercantilism to capitalism, which became the governing economic form in the late eighteenth century. There is no doubt that London prospered on the backs of slaves, and port cities like Bristol and, particularly, Liverpool ascended as their merchants' pockets filled with gold. According to Jack Watson, for instance, from 1783 to 1793 Liverpool merchants sold over 300,000 slaves with a net profit to the town of about £10 on each one.

At the same time, the west coast of Africa was plundered. It has been estimated – and their can be no way of knowing the exact numbers – that over the course of two centuries twenty million people were forcibly removed from their homeland. In their place, the traders left guns, trinkets, rum and other worthless bribes. Africa, as well as the Caribbean, was mercilessly exploited by European 'progress' during the seventeenth and eighteenth centuries.

While England was adopting a system of slavery in her colonies to satisfy her needs, English society itself had been very slowly evolving toward the system of 'free' labour synonymous with capitalism. This labour force, however, lacked any access to productive property and had to sell its labour to the owners of the means of production. But as Sidney Mintz describes in *Sweetness and Power*, these two radically different patterns of labour extraction, of Jamaican slave and English labourer, were intimately connected by sugar in several ways. First, by the mechanisms of the triangular trade itself: finished goods were sold to Africa, African slaves to the Americas, and sugar to the mother country and her importing neighbours. Thus, the wealth created by slaves returned to Britain and in the factories of its evolving industrial sector, poor English people made the products – cloths, tools, torture instruments – that were consumed by the slaves who were themselves consumed in the creation of wealth. Sugar, therefore, was mistress both of the poor of Britain and the slaves of Jamaica.

Secondly, during the second half of the eighteenth century, poor people in England actually began to consume more and more sugar themselves, as its supply increased and sugar products were differentiated from molasses and rum to other crystalline sugar varieties and syrups. Throughout the seventeenth and early eighteenth centuries, sugar had been enjoyed by the rich: it was only after a major fall in its price in the nineteenth century that it profoundly altered the meagre diet of the working class. But before then, poor people were beginning to consume sugar as a sweetener in drinks made from the other colonial foodstuffs – tea, coffee and chocolate – that were also gaining popularity at the time.

Served hot and sweetened, these beverages were particularly welcome to those in the factory system, with its emphasis on the saving of time and the poorly-paid and exhausting jobs it offered women and children. So too was treacle, smeared on bread to replace a meal. Between 1650 and 1800, Mintz suggests that British sugar consumption had probably increased by 2,500%, as the famous English penchant for sweetness, and for a 'cuppa', took hold. This transformation linked the consumption habits of every English person to the colonies of the Empire; the bag of sugar on the supermarket shelf today with the lives of those in Gaythorne.

The beginning of the end for Jamaica: competition, war and debt

In the colony of Jamaica, meanwhile, slave rebellion was only one of several contenders for the planter classes' attention at the end of the eighteenth century. Many were experiencing serious economic problems induced by war and new competition. Until the defeat of Napoleon in 1815, Anglo-French conflict over colonial territory had a debilitating effect on the island. Trade was interrupted, resulting in loss of revenue; slaves and estate equipment were in short supply; there was conflict between local governors and commanders; and Britain increased both its taxes on the planters, and the export duties on sugar, to pay for troops. Even when the wars gave the plantation owners a momentary advantage by making sugar scarce in Europe so that prices were high, there was a counter-balancing disadvantage that this only stimulated the Europeans to seek supplies elsewhere. In the late eighteenth century, sugarcane plantations were established in Mauritius, Java and the Philippines. Moreover, Germany, who had failed to get a place in the Caribbean sun, was developing its own sugar beet industry – indicating that that place was no longer necessary. No longer could sugar only be grown in the tropics. The world sugar market that chapter two described was beginning to develop.

The development of alternative sugars

As Hobhouse relates, during the Napoleonic Wars French sugar ships had run the blockade of the Royal Navy in the West Indies. They also suffered the loss of 100,000 tons of sugar a year which had previously come from Saint-Domingue. Against this background of shortage and high prices Napoleon became aware of the botanical researches of Andrew Sigimond Margraf, of the Berlin Academy. Margraf had discovered that there were significant quantities of sugar in carrots, parsnips, and above all sea beet, a cousin of the beetroot. However, it was not until 1801, long after

Margraf's death, that any sugar production took place commercially. Encouraged by the high wartime price of sugar, the first selection and crossing of roots for sugar took place. Within ten years, the beet industry was born, and in many continental countries, notably France, it was developed with subsidy after the peace in 1815. Within fifteen years, beet sugar was threatening the tropical trade.

Serious competitors for Jamaica's supremacy were also to be found closer to home. After the Declaration of Independence in Britain's North American colonies in 1776, Jamaica lost its monopoly over the American market and was left face to face with their French rivals, and in particular Saint-Domingue (the western part of the island of Hispaniola, later to comprise Haiti and the Dominican Republic). Jamaica was suffering from declining soil fertility, duplicating the history of Barbados – while Saint Domingue, with more space and more fertile soil, was said to be able to produce five times the amount of sugarcane per acre than Jamaica. The British market remained protected but the American market was lost – and by the 1780s Saint Domingue was supplying most of the needs of continental Europe as well.

Paradoxically, Jamaica was losing ground even in the market of the mother country itself. It was Britain that was emerging from centuries of struggle as the most forceful colonising power in the West Indies, and various treaties had added sugar-growing islands to the British Empire. Jamaican planters therefore were faced with new and more productive competition from these other islands, which enjoyed the same privileged access to the British sweet tooth.

The fear of insurrection that obsessed the Jamaican plantocracy was about to manifest itself on another Caribbean island. The Haitian slave revolution broke out in full force in 1791, two years after a better-known cataclysm in France. As Roger Plant describes, it was infinitely more bloodthirsty, with widespread atrocities on both sides reducing Saint-Domingue to anarchy and chaos before the new Republic of Haiti was officially born in 1804. It was also a complex struggle, with more than oppressed black slaves and imperious white masters as antagonists and interest groups. The catalyst to the revolution was actually the demands of the free mulatto population of Saint Domingue, seeking the rights that accrued to them from the revolutionary proclamation in far-off Paris. But as violence grew, their demands served to fan the flames of a slave rebellion that ended white supremacy once and for all.

According to the *Code Noir,* the free mulattos were technically regarded as full French citizens. They had property rights, but faced discrimination everywhere else. So they took up arms against the metropolitan elite in the name of freedom, equality and fraternity. Slaves joined in and Civil War ensued. In the midst of this Napoleon took over France and decided to recover Saint-Domingue. The ensuing battle resulted in the massacre of all white men and women by the victorious rebels, and the new Republic of Haiti was born in 1804. Not only French supremacy but the sugar economy came to an abrupt end. In 1781 it had exported 930,000 *quintales* of raw sugar; by 1818, down to 55,000. By 1825, Haitian independence was recognised by France, ending a 130-year period of colonial domination that had brought vast profits to their sugar planters and untold misery to hundreds of thousands of black slaves.

Revolution in St. Domingue, and the capture by the British of yet more sugar growing areas, might have been expected to bring the Jamaican planters some relief. The revolution destroyed the principle competitor; and as Britain had come near to having a monopoly of West Indian sugar islands, international buyers might have been expected to come to the British for their sugar. But at this moment, the Spanish in Cuba turned more seriously to sugar production, centuries after their initial experiments in the Caribbean. And as they made considerable inroads into the American market, the French followed the German example and encouraged the widespread planting of sugar beet at home. As profitability in the Jamaican sugar industry declined, many planters fell into debt. Moreover, revolution in Haiti had increased their terror of insurrection by their own slaves, and more and more abandoned their estates. The island's apogee was over. Its position as the focus of the Caribbean sugar industry was lost for ever in the face of new competition and changing circumstances of trade – the circumstances which history now repeats two hundred years later, to bring the sugar industries of the Caribbean islands as a whole to the brink of extinction.

The period of war and change in the late eighteenth century Caribbean coincided with the Age of Enlightenment in Europe. New ideas stirred and many old ones were challenged. In 1776, Adam Smith vigorously attacked mercantilism when he published *The Wealth of Nations*, a pro-free trade tome that had a profound effect on economic ideas. In 1787, Thomas Clarkson published his *Essay on Slavery* and helped to found the Society for Effecting the Abolition of the Slave Trade. The West Indian lobby for a time successfully frustrated all abolitionist legislation in Britain – but the foundations of slave-based sugar production were beginning to crumble and in the nineteenth century, would turn to dust.

The end of the slave system: nineteenth century humanity?

The emancipation of slaves in the British West Indies was at last achieved in 1838; the French followed in 1848 and the Spanish in Cuba, who resisted attempts for reform, followed finally in 1884. The drive to abolition had taken place in and around English Parliament, and had been a long and bitter contest between the West Indian planters, humanitarian interests, and a new group of British capitalists who had nothing in common with the West Indian lobby. Abolition is generally accredited to the work of famous humanitarian campaigners such as Wilberforce and Buxton, and indeed, there is no doubt that their efforts were responsible for the wider acknowledgement of the inhumanity of slavery. But it seems more likely that the collapse of the slave system was basically the result of the fact that it had lost its former importance to the metropolitan economy. In 1885 beet overtook cane in the total world sugar trade in sugar. And, as Eric Williams has written, there were now new industrialists and businessmen in England who had commercial interests in textiles, iron, coal and pottery, and could see new possibilities for trade to replace the profits of slavery. Ships could carry cotton rather than slaves into the docks of Liverpool.

The decline of British exports to the Caribbean had coincided with the increasing unprofitability of British West Indian production, and by the mid nineteenth century the days of mercantilism were clearly over. The final blow to the British planter class came when the protectionism that they had been afforded under the Navigation Acts and the Sugar Duties began to be eroded under the attacks of the free-trade advocates. The Sugar Duties, which subsidised the British West Indian planters, held the prices of sugar in Britain artificially high; and now that sugar could be bought more cheaply from Spanish producers in the Caribbean who were still using slaves, or from the cane plantations of the East or, increasingly, from beet producers in Europe itself, such protection was anathema to the disciples of Adam Smith. The islands had lost their function as the providers of capital to England; now, they were no longer needed to produce the low cost food substitute for the English labouring classes.

Sugar had become so important that supply could not be allowed to depend upon the mercantilist-nationalist arrangements that had formerly controlled it. As Sidney Mintz writes, by removing barriers to 'free' trade – by making it possible for the world's cheapest sugars to reach the widest possible market in Britain – the leading sectors of British capitalism sold out the planter class.

For three centuries sugar had shaped the formation of Caribbean economies and societies. From Hispaniola to Barbados, to Jamaica, and to Saint Domingue, each island had in turn had its moment as the most important cane producer in the Caribbean. Now, as the external structures of the plantation system were removed, it seemed likely that the region's encounter with the sugar industry would be over. But almost incredibly, as the nineteenth century progressed, and the era of colonialism and slavery began to fade, new supports appeared to keep the structures of plantation society in place.

Alongside the abolition for slavery came the re-introduction of indentured labour to work in the cane fields, and under this system migration to the Caribbean from the East completed the region's ethnological transformation. And with the theoretical freedom of Emancipation came new measures to prevent freed slaves from acquiring their own land, thus curtailing the establishment of either rural communities independent of the plantation or an indigenous agriculture. All in all, during the nineteenth century, the thumbprint of sugar was indented ever more deeply into the Caribbean, as the fate of the region and its sugar industry became ever more intertwined.

Struggle and change

The new influx of indentured labour to replace the slaves on the sugar estates started immediately after emancipation and continued well into the twentieth century. Vast numbers of people came from India and China, and smaller numbers from Europe and Africa. Details as to the terms of contract varied but the system differed little, in its basic pattern, from the indentured labour of two centuries earlier. The new contracts were usually for a period of five years, and they included provision for the labourer's small wages and for the return journey home. Towards the end of the nineteenth century, such a return came to be discouraged and as an alternative it became usual to offer smallholdings to the workers when the

Indentured labourers from India

term of contract ended. Indenture, however, smacked of slavery and the British Government of India banned further contracts in 1916 – although by then well over 500,000 Indians had made the journey to the Caribbean and only 100,000 had returned.

The impact of the new immigration varied between the islands. The Jamaican sugar industry had by now substantially declined, and so only forty thousand Indians went to the remaining plantations that were buoyant enough to be able to afford new labour. More than 100,000 Chinese went to Cuba, conversely, where demand was soaring as estates expanded. Post-emancipation migration to the Dominican Republic was largely European; and in neighbouring Haiti the sugar industry had failed completely after the Revolution and there were no new immigrants at all. Neither, moreover, were indentured labourers needed in Barbados. In this small island, the plantation entirely dominated the landscape and the ex-slaves had no choice but to stay and work for wages in the cane fields. For this reason, paradoxically, Barbados, unlike Jamaica, saw an increase in its sugar production after emancipation.

Under the plantation sugar economy based on slavery, the Caribbean region had presented a fairly uniform picture of land use and settlement.

Table 5
The historical perspective – production (000 metric tonnes)

	Cuba	British West Indies	Dominican Republic	Puerto Rico	French Possessions	Total	World Total	Caribbean share of world %
1850	223	100	n.a.	50	28	401	1,202	33
1900	284	126	53*	63	62	588	11,259	5
1920	3,729	128	168*	446	53	4,524	16,831	27
1940	2,441	426	394*	832	153	4,246	30,429	14
1960	5,862	889	1,112	933	302	9,098	59,767	15
1980	6,805	521	1,013	n.a.	n.a.	8,339	84,631	10
1990	8,445	426	590	n.a.	n.a.	9,461	110,959	9
1999	3,875	377	421	n.a.	n.a.	4,673	136,325	3

* exports
n.a. not available

Source: A C Hannah, Head, Economics and Statistics Division ISO, London (International Sugar Organisation), 2001

Now, after emancipation, inter-island variations began to appear, according to how much land was available for the freed slaves to occupy. On islands where sugarcane dominated the landscape, an existence independent of the plantation was largely impossible, but in Jamaica and others where there was hilly land that had remained unplanted, the freed slaves struggled fiercely to rid themselves of the chains that had tied them to sugar. In Jamaica, freed slaves quickly 'reconstituted' themselves to form a 'peasant' sector on the steep slopes and thin soils of the mountainous interior of the island, or on the edges of the fertile lowlands dominated by cane – building upon the production that they had undertaken during slavery, and producing food crops for subsistence and for the domestic market. This settlement forms the basis of the present patterns of small farming today.

From the very beginning, however, the powers that be did their utmost to thwart the fledgling indigenous agriculture and preserve the islands' position as sugar-cane monocultures. Land, obviously, was key. In Jamaica, for example, the planters went to extreme measures to control it: refusing to sell small parcels of estate land or charging exorbitant prices; levying land taxes; and adopting strict legislation against squatting. The 'peasantry', therefore, was ultimately unable to remain independent of the plantation. Hunger forced people to seek wage employment on the estates, alongside other landless labourers, and over time they began to grow sugar cane to sell. Ignored by the mother country, Jamaica and her sister-islands remained tied to the sugar industry, with their people doomed, as Mintz describes, to straddle two economic adaptations – as reconstituted peasants and as rural proletarians – neither of which could become economically secure.

In this way, the patterns and problems that are still manifest today in the rural Caribbean were established. As chapter one described, in the remaining areas of contemporary sugar-cane cultivation in Jamaica, many rural people live in poverty and are forced to labour in the cane fields, grow cane to sell to the estate, and farm their own minuscule plots of land for their subsistence. Small farming remains in perpetual conflict with plantation agriculture, losing out to the latter over land resources and capital investment. And as a result Jamaica, and the Caribbean region as a whole, has been unable to become self-sufficient in domestic food production. Until the present, agriculture has remained export-oriented, and people from rural communities have been forced to look to the towns, cities and overseas for their livelihoods.

Vacuum pans, corporate capital and Cuba – nineteenth century expansion

Despite Emancipation and the near-collapse of the Jamaican sugar industry, during the nineteenth century sugar production actually increased in the Caribbean region as a whole. At the forefront of this expansion was Spanish-held Cuba. At first, Cuba's expansion, like that of Barbados, Jamaica and Hispaniola before it, was based on virgin soil – with the added advantage of slave labour, long after its French and English competitors had been forced to abandon it. In addition, the island's greater size gave it an advantage over the smaller territories in the region, and also aided its position at the forefront of the adoption of new technology. After centuries of unchanging practice, an 'industrial revolution' of the sugar industry got underway, as the technologies of mechanised sugar beet production made their way to the Caribbean from Europe. At the beginning of the nineteenth century, Cuban sugar output was less than half that of Jamaica; by the end, as Jack Watson writes, it was almost four times the total production of the British West Indies.

The modernisation of the traditional system of cane sugar production started during the first half of the century, at a moment when it became urgent for planters to reduce their costs of production in order to withstand the aggressive competition from beet sugar. Steam power, horizontal grinding mills and the vacuum pan (to accelerate the clarification of cane liquid) were slowly introduced and during the latter half of the century, mills began to be centralised for greater efficiency. This process was eventually region-wide, but most rapid and far-reaching in Cuba. Production on the island expanded steadily throughout the century, and plantations were very large by Caribbean standards – more than 10,000 acres each by the 1850s. Moreover, with the rise of industrial chemistry, the quality of the chemical control in the manufacture of sugar was greatly improved, affecting the cane industry after about 1870.

Only a large enterprise could afford to maintain a resident chemist, as indeed only such an enterprise could afford an engineering staff to keep the ever more sophisticated machinery in order. By the end of the nineteenth century in Cuba, some of the *centrales* had grown very large indeed; according to David Watts, for example, in 1890 the *Costania Central* had become the largest sugar factory in the world, processing 19

500 tons of sugar alone – a quantity which was virtually equivalent to that of the whole of Jamaica at the time.

The British producers meanwhile largely clung to the eighteenth century pattern of separate factories for individual estates, being slow to realise the benefits of centralisation, or too poor to procure them. However, as most of the smaller family-run enterprises collapsed, so amalgamations took place – in Trelawny in Jamaica for example, the number of estates collapsed from 89 to less than half this number.

The capital needed for the central factory was generally beyond the resources of any private investor and the cost of technology was at a new level of magnitude. Along with this production zenith, therefore, came the first penetration of corporate capital, which again was pre-eminent in Cuba. In the second half of the nineteenth century, American money became heavily involved in the Cuban sugar industry and economy; it also began to penetrate into the plantation interests of the wider Caribbean. For Cuba, this was a profound historical turn, setting in motion a chain of events that, in the next century, would have global political-economic consequences. And for the region as a whole, it heralded the beginnings of a new, American, imperialism. Not only was this the start of corporate dominance which would develop into the penetration of multinational companies, explored in the previous chapter; it was also the beginning of the relationship between US foreign policy and US capital, which would have profound effects for the Caribbean region in the twentieth century.

The strong links between US big business and the country's foreign policy were forged during the last decades of the nineteenth century, and were the culmination of the paternalism and expansionism that had defined the century for the United States. As Jenny Pearce writes, the Monroe Doctrine of 1823 had established the right of the US to 'protect' Latin America, declaring that interference by any European power would be considered an unfriendly act towards the US; later, the phrase 'manifest destiny' symbolised the belief that the US should carry its particular brand of economic, social and political organisation westwards. By 1890, this expansion was almost complete within the US. Moreover, by now, its population was greater than that of any single European country, and its production of steel, coal and iron was also outpacing Europe. Giant monopoly firms had emerged with surplus capital for export, and there were now new wider ideas of empire. Cuba was the first target for this expansion.

At the end of the nineteenth century, Cuba remained the brightest jewel in the Caribbean crown. Jamaica, its predecessor, had dropped from the list of the top six Caribbean sugar producers; the Dominican Republic, meanwhile was once again a major producer, and Barbados had also revitalised its industry. Sugar cane had established itself as the *raison d'être* of the region, from Puerto Rico to Guadeloupe; three centuries of colonialism had made sure that it produced little else. In the twentieth century, the people of the Caribbean would wrestle with this legacy, and attempt to establish viable independent economies, as European colonialism gave way to the formation of new nation states. But, as we see in chapter five, they would do so against the odds.

Chapter Five

Sugar in the Twentieth Century
The King is dead! Long live the King!

'What was the way forward? To go forward you had to recognise the depth of the trap in which you were caught. Hence, 'forward' became not so much a matter of marching on level ground, but had to begin with the question how to climb up out of the trap...'
Michael Manley, Struggle on the Periphery, 1982

In 1897 the West India Royal Commission reported the findings of its investigation into the economic problems of the British-held islands in the Caribbean. The abject rural poverty that it had documented was blamed on the collapse of the sugar industry, and the Commission called upon the Government to persuade its continental neighbours to abandon their financial support of sugar beet. Moreover, it called for the settlement in the West Indies 'of the native population as proprietors and cultivators of small portions of land' for the prospect of 'moderate prosperity and political stability'. The first objective was successfully met, and the sugar industry of the British West Indies revived during the first half of the twentieth century; the second, however, remained an elusive goal.

But most importantly, Joseph Chamberlain's Royal Commission provided a foretaste of the apparently insoluble developmental problems ahead. In assuming that the sugar industry alone would be unable to bring prosperity to the islands, it set the scene for the twentieth century. How could the brutal association of the sugar industry and poverty be overcome? And most importantly, how could the economic dependence upon sugar cane itself be alleviated?

Despite its revival, during the early decades of the twentieth century the sugar industry in the British and French West Indies was the poor relation to the vast plantations of the islands of the former Spanish Caribbean. Under increasing American corporate penetration, sugar production in Cuba, Puerto Rico and the Dominican Republic escalated.

So too did the United States' political involvement in these islands. What began under the auspices of 'financial management' and republican 'good neighbourliness' appeared quickly to become imperialist hegemony; and after the Second World War, and a revolution in Cuba, the politics of the Cold War permeated the region. All of this affected the sugar industry. The United States opened and closed its market for sugar from 'favoured' and 'less favoured' Caribbean islands, according to geopolitics. Trade, like aid, became a political tool. Similar manoeuvring over recent decades has influenced the contemporary trade arrangements that chapter two explored, which presently threaten the survival of the industry.

In the latter half of the century, development strategies reflecting different economic philosophies have been variously applied to the islands of the Caribbean. All the newly independent nation states were anxious to diversify away from dependence on sugar production and its historical associations with slavery. Earlier centuries of plantation agriculture had given the region a uniform economic structure, tempered only by physical geography and 'small farm' development. Now, through decades of development planning, more significant economic differences emerged.

With varying degrees of success, the islands managed to expand their economies – and develop light industrial sectors, mineral exports and tourist industries. The export of their people, too, generated important income in the form of remittances sent home from abroad. In most islands, the importance of the sugar industry decreased; in a few, it disappeared altogether. But even though its contribution to Gross National Product fell, sugar remained a backbone of the rural economy across much of the region – where the timeless conflict between the plantation and domestic agriculture lingers. This, as we have seen, is the focus of a contemporary crisis of the Caribbean.

Over the last two decades, the debt crisis and its accompanying impositions of neoliberalism have reorientated the sugar industry in the region's economy. Under structural adjustment the debt-ridden islands have been encouraged to privatise their sugar industries and expand their exports, to raise the revenues to pay back their loans – although this approach is at odds with the impending trade reforms which will affect international sugar markets. Although the crisis of the Caribbean sugar industry is connected to these global developments, its local circumstances vary enormously from island to island – from Cuba, with a history as one of the world's most important producers, to Barbados, which continues to sink into global insignificance as a commodity producer. As we explore in this chapter, Jamaica, Barbados, Cuba and the Dominican Republic each face a 'personalised' crisis, according to their own histories. And by understanding this – the idiosyncrasies of their struggles during the twentieth century – we can gain a clearer perspective of the possibilities for the 'post-sugar' era.

Goodbye Alfonso, hello Uncle Sam: the American sugar kingdom

In some ways, the United State's intervention in the Caribbean during the first decades of the twentieth century was a positive force of development. The first recipient of its attentions was Cuba where, after a century of misgovernment and repression, a bitter revolution against the Spanish had begun. By this time, American capital had become heavily involved in the Cuban economy – particularly in the sugar industry – and in 1898 the United States decided to 'liberate' the island. Under the American military rule which lasted until 1902, the US was able to restore prosperity to their sugar interests and impose order more widely: a new constitution was drawn up, improvements were made to the administrative and educational systems, and public works and new standards of sanitation were instituted. Almost overnight yellow fever was wiped out.

However, American intervention was not a simple act of charity. As Eric Williams notes, the Caribbean itself was to become the American Mediterranean. As the Assistant Secretary of State pronounced in 1904, 'no picture of our future is complete which does not contemplate and comprehend the US as the dominant power in the Caribbean Sea'. In return for Independence, the Cubans were forced to sign the Military Approbation Bill, better known as the Platt Amendment. This authorised the US the right to keep a 'watchful eye' on the financial management of the island's government and to establish military bases in Guantanamo Bay and elsewhere. Moreover, when law and order broke down, American troops intervened again and occupied Cuba in 1906 and 1909, and from 1917 to 1923; but otherwise, the US was able to direct its management of Cuba for the next fifty years from Washington. American economic and political domination had been secured without the seizure of a colony, and Cuba became the model for the new regional imperialism of the twentieth century. The Platt Amendment was to govern the United States' relations with Cuba until the advent of Fidel Castro.

117

The Spanish-American war brought to an end Spain's vast empire in the Americas and, after its 'liberation' of Cuba, the United States took 'responsibility' for Spain's other colonies. In 1901 Puerto Rico became a 'non-incorporated territory' of the United States; after this, the neighbourliness stretched towards the Caribbean Republics of Haiti and the Dominican Republic. United States' marines occupied Haiti between 1914 and 1934, and the Dominican Republic between 1916 and 1924. In accordance with a new interpretation of the Monroe Doctrine, the US felt it had a mission to teach their neighbours to elect 'good men', and to be better accountants; on both islands, they were unfortunately successful in installing despotic dictators.

American intervention in the Dominican Republic and Haiti began with the collection of debt by gunboat. Like other countries in the region, the islands had borrowed from European and United States' creditors in order to build railroads and ports. In 1904 the government of the Dominican Republic defaulted on its payments to an American financial company, and the US took over the collection of Customs Duties and the country's finances. In this way, as Jenny Pearce writes, the economic and political became ever more intimately connected in United States foreign policy.

Of course, this relationship influenced the sugar industry in these islands. In Cuba, the investment of US corporate capital into the plantations in the late nineteenth century had later necessitated the need for political action – now conversely, with Puerto Rico, the Dominican Republic and Haiti under the management of home-grown military power, the American sugar corporations were able to expand across the Caribbean Sea. King Sugar could increase his grip on the islands where the American influence was strong.

For the first half of the twentieth century, the American sugar kingdom was spectacularly successful. According to Eric Williams, the period between 1897 and 1930 saw an enormous concentration of plantations under the stimulus of the United States' capital investment. The combined acreage of six plantations operated by the Cuban American Sugar Company totalled a half million acres; that of the nine plantations of the Cuban Atlantic Sugar Company 400,000. Symbolic of the new age was the United Fruit Company. The backing for its control of 93,000 acres of cane land in Cuba was its various properties in the Caribbean, Central and South America, the Canary Islands, Europe and the US, totalling at the beginning of 1941 over three million acres. As Williams notes, its sugar production in Cuba was part of a huge empire which controlled 65% of the world's supply of bananas, included a tourist hotel in Jamaica, embraced its own fleet of cargo and passenger vessels, and dominated 40% of the entire rolling stock of the International Railways of Central America. In short, as chapter three described, sugar had become very big business.

What was true of Cuba was also true of Puerto Rico, and the Dominican Republic presented a similar pattern – where two American companies owned 250,000 acres between them. Large plantations were paralleled by large factories; centralisation in the factory paralleled centralisation in the field. In Cuba, the processes that began in the nineteenth century were intensified – and pursued too in the other islands dominated by the United States. According to Williams, by 1930, Puerto Rico was producing almost a million tonnes of sugar, compared with the 50,000 it had harvested under the Spanish; in Haiti, under the stimulus of US capital, sugar increased from 3% of total exports for the decade 1916 to 1926, to nearly 20% in 1939; and in the Dominican Republic, output increased tenfold between 1903 and 1939. The links between these islands and the American market were cemented.

As sugar production increased, so did its overall dominance of the island's economies. The monoculture typical of Caribbean history was recreated. During the early decades of the twentieth century, sugar constituted more than 80% of Cuba's exports, and more than 70% of the Dominican Republic's. Building upon the inequities of the past, the domestic economies were further distorted: the export of other crops such as coffee plummeted, the demand for lands led to further overcrowding on the small holdings which yielded little more than subsistence on the edges of plantations, and the appalling wages paid to labourers set the pattern for inadequate standards of living. But most importantly, the company plantations were export enclaves. While the sugar industry of the so-called American Mediterranean boomed, little or no contribution was made to the indigenous economic development of the islands. Like a record stuck in a groove, the same old tune of the previous centuries played on.

In an attempt to bestow some organisation on its domestic and import policy, in 1934 the United States established a quota system for sugar imports from the Caribbean and elsewhere. Quotas were set for each country on the basis of an assessment of the quantity of sugar required –

this, together with the price, varied yearly. This system remained in force until 1948 when the Sugar Act was implemented – but exporting countries have been vulnerable to the varying quantity and value of their US sugar quota until the present.

Poor relations: the sugar industry in the colonial West Indies

During the first few decades of the twentieth century, the sugar industry of the British colonies was a hopelessly inadequate opponent of its American rivals. The 1897 West India Royal Commission had expressed the opinion that 'under any circumstances that can at present be foreseen, the days of very large or excessive profits from the sugar-cane industry appear to us to have passed away.' Sugar cultivation and manufacture on the scale that had resulted from United States penetration called for a colossal investment in capital, which only the United States could afford.

Barbados was typical. The land in plantations totalled 52,000 acres out of a total of 66,000 – although tiny in comparison to its American rivals, it was still a plantation economy. Sugar constituted 95% of exports. But only nine of its plantations were over 500 acres in size. In Jamaica, moreover, each estate had an average size of only 187 acres, and total production between all 140 of them was just 14,000 tons of sugar. The British West Indian sugar industry, like the small cane farmer of the Spanish Caribbean, was a casualty of the multinational corporation – who had primed the size, productivity and efficiency of its competitors and, as an added extra, satisfied the American markets.

The 1897 Commission had called for agricultural diversification in the British West Indies as a matter of the highest priority and greatest urgency. It acknowledged that 'the representatives of the sugar industry in the West Indies have had special means... of putting pressure on the Home Government to secure attention to their views and wishes' but warned them that 'so long as they (the islands) remain dependent upon sugar, their position can never be secure'. Alongside this it encouraged land reform and settlement, as a means to allow rural people the right to indigenous agriculture and self-determination away from the confines of the plantation.

The situation for the mass of the rural people in the West Indian colonies was one of utter deprivation: they struggled to survive through their own agriculture and whatever work they could get on the estates. Those who

120

Wind Mill Sugar Estate, Barbados, c.1930s   *Picture courtesy of John Gilmore*

were landless were destitute. But this pre-war period was also a moment of historic opportunity. Despite the constraints upon land and capital, land use and agro-exports in Jamaica, at least, were diversifying considerably. As a result of the labours of rural people in the production of bananas, coffee and citrus, sugar constituted just 15% of exports – the monoculture of a pure plantation economy had been substantially eroded. It was a pivotal moment, when American corporations could be thanked for their success, and the prospect of real emancipation could be grasped. But by 1929, when the Olivier Sugar Commission reported, it was clear that this moment had been lost.

Until the outbreak of the First World War, production in Jamaica remained very low. In 1913, it had fallen to 5,000 tons, which was less than in any year since 1710. But at the beginning of the century, when the crisis was at its worst, the industry experienced another period of profound change. In apparent response to the work of the West India Royal Committee of 1897, the various systems of bounties on beet sugar production were phased out. Although this did not result in an immediate increase in sugar prices, removal of 'unfair' competition in Europe improved the industry's prospects.

121

Meanwhile, investment was encouraged by the home government. Ignorant of the need to support further diversification, deaf to the calls for land reform and blind to the needs of domestic agriculture, direct intervention was made by those in power to ensure the preservation of the sugar industry – provided by way of government guarantee of interest on the capital of any company investing in the island.

The fortunes of the sugar industry in the British West Indies began to change significantly following the destruction of the European sugar beet industry during World War One. As markets for cane improved, sugar production began to increase and by 1917 in Jamaica, production had reached 32,000 tons. Moreover, during the war and subsequently, amalgamations and the establishment of central factories continued in Jamaica. In 1920, a dozen new estate names were included in the list of properties which, together with the extension of acreage more than balanced – for the first time in about a hundred years – the loss of abandoned estates. And the average size of plantations between 1920 and 1930 had nearly doubled.

Despite the apparent 'bottoming out' of the crisis, however, the condition of sugar production remained critical. Following a fall in the price of sugar on the world market, representations had been made to the British Government by all the West Indian colonies, as to their depressed condition. The West Indian Sugar Commission of 1929/30 was duly appointed to repeat the exercise undertaken thirty years previously. It documented the hardship endured by those working in the industry, and the unlikely prospects of its continued survival under world market conditions. Again, the Commission paid particular attention to the need for land reform. But its outcome was only a continuation of the pattern of intervention in the industry that had been established in 1902.

In 1930 the Imperial Government commenced the issue of what were known as Special Colonial Preference Certificates, offering a protected British market to the colonial sugar producers. Intended to maintain existing manufacturers in production, they were the forerunners of the modern day preferential markets that until now have kept the Jamaican and Barbadian sugar industries alive. As Cuba and the Dominican Republics had their markets in the United States, so the British-held islands could sell to the mother country: here unwittingly, were sown the seeds of the crisis that would re-emerge seventy years later.

Escaping the plantation/small farm conflict

As the sugar industry was kick-started, the landless rural labourer and struggling small farmer continued to struggle. The Olivier Commission which had recorded that 'it is impossible to expect any sound permanent development unless steps are taken to enable the small cultivators to obtain and possess their land in freehold' had also acknowledged that if the sugar planters 'encouraged such action which in their belief, must tend to diminish their labour supply, they would be cutting away the branch upon which they sit.' In the conflict between the plantation and the independent small farmer – which had begun at emancipation – the former was winning throughout the Caribbean.

Unable to acquire adequate land or employment, many workers were forced to migrate. Just as in the previous century, Asian immigrants had sent their earnings home, these migrant workers began the pattern of temporary and permanent migrations that have persisted until today, in order to support their families. Before restrictions were imposed in 1924, many West Indians emigrated to the United States; and before the first World War, there was work to be had in building the Panama Canal. Most importantly, the islands with buoyant sugar industries attracted workers from islands where the sugar industry flagged. Cuba acted as a powerful magnet, for the gigantic expansion of the sugar industry required more labour than was available locally, and this was true too, on a smaller scale, of the Dominican Republic. In Cuba, this importation was called 'swallow' immigration, as the majority of workers could come only for the sugar season and then return home.

According to Eric Williams, the average annual exodus from Jamaica, largely to Cuba, was 10,000 for the half century before 1935; the average annual remittances sent to Jamaica from overseas in the 1930s reached $600,000. 'Panama money', moreover, remitted to Barbados by Barbadians abroad, totalled in 1930 nearly $1,250,000 – a sum nearly equal to one third of the value of Barbadian exports for that year. Such earnings became a very significant part of the survival strategies of rural communities, and these travels a memorable aspect of peoples' lives. For instance, the very elderly men in Gaythorne, described in chapter one, told of the conditions of their work in the sugar industry in Cuba in their youth, and how the money that they earned allowed them to 'get a start'. Women spoke commonly of the unspoken commitments which ensured that they received a remittance upon which they and their children could survive. In more contemporary times, these opportunities to work in the sugar industry overseas have been replicated by the United States' farmwork programme, which recruits ten to fifteen thousand workers a year, mostly from Jamaica, on temporary contracts to cut cane.

The 1930s in the Caribbean colonies: lull before the storm

At the beginning of the 1930s, the sugar industry in the British and French West Indies was still small in size – indeed, it was a sad reflection of the lack of alternative economic opportunities that it had managed to maintain such a dominant position in the islands' economies. According to Eric Williams, for example, in the British West Indies 33% of the population of St. Kitts and Antigua was directly employed in the sugar industry, and 20% of Barbadians. Sixty seven per cent of the area of Martinique, 50% of Barbados and 20% of Jamaica were planted with cane. For most islands, little change had taken place between the West India Royal Commission of 1897 and the Olivier Sugar Commission of 1928. Sugar and its by-products constituted 97% of total Barbadian exports in 1896 and 95% in 1928; in Jamaica, its importance remained steady at 18%.

Only in a few selected islands had its dominance faded over this period as other economic sectors developed: in Trinidad, where oil had been discovered, its proportion of the island's exports had been more than halved; and in St. Lucia and St. Vincent, where the sugar plantations were being replaced by bananas, it had fallen sharply. But in the larger islands, meanwhile, multinational corporations were investing in the sugar industry. Foreign capital moved further to restructure and solidify its control through the amalgamation and centralisation of factory operations and the establishment of immense factory farms.

Desperate poverty and under-employment continued on the plantations. The condition of the sugar worker reflected the harsh realities of colonialism: malnourished and hungry people were underweight, short and inadequately housed, and they suffered from malaria, hookworm and tuberculosis. A Barbados Commission, for example, reported that the price of locally grown vegetables was often so high as to be beyond the modest means of the labourer, who was therefore reduced to a diet of imported rice and cornmeal. Many could only obtain intermittent work. Both the government and private employers adopted the policy of

A planter's residence, Barbados, c.1920s   Picture courtesy of John Gilmore

'rotational employment', where a worker was taken on for a fortnight and then discharged to make way for another. The trading concerns maintained their high dividends and comfortable salaries of the higher grades of employees on the basis of impossibly low wages for the mass of the workers.

With characteristic ingrained prejudice, the sugar planters of the British West Indies tried to impress upon the Olivier Sugar Commission that it was the workers who refused to work; the vicious habit of drinking inferior rum on Sundays, they postulated, was responsible for abstention from work on Mondays. Other witnesses, as Williams writes, however, blamed the old industrial theory that it was necessary to maintain a constant supply of cheap labour and that, therefore, no labourer must be too highly paid or given too much employment. Nor, for that matter, too much education: the rights of the rural child to a good education were subjugated to the privileges of the planter class, who presumed the rigours of literacy and numeracy to be irrelevant to the needs of the sugar estate.

The Great Depression of the era, experienced throughout Europe and America, added to the hardship. As the price of sugar fell lower than at any time since the 1890s, wages were reduced further still and jobs terminated throughout the Caribbean. The sugar industry set the scene for other sectors of the economy. Unlike the slow recovery experienced in the advanced countries, the effects of the Depression lingered tenaciously in the Caribbean. When the safety valve of migration proved inadequate, such campaigning individuals as Marcus Garvey joined the voices of protest and frustration, as the West Indies erupted into strikes, demonstrations and riots.

Strikes on the sugar plantations spread around the islands and agricultural workers were joined by dockers and industrial labourers in the demand for better jobs and higher wages. Strikes in Jamaica in 1934 were followed by action in St. Kitts in 1935; the worst of the disorders, however, were in 1937 and 1938, when there was a sugar strike in St. Lucia and Barbados workers rioted in Bridgetown, and in Jamaica at the new Tate and Lyle factory. Every British Governor, as Williams recalls, called for warships, marines and aeroplanes. But these were formative years for the British West Indies: out of the social upheaval, trade unionism and nationalism emerged and coalesced, the political parties of the future were conceived, and the British, unfortunately, developed the habit of arresting the political leaders of the post-war years.

The disturbances at the Frome sugar factory in Jamaica are perhaps the most memorable, sketched in the personal histories of elderly men in Gaythorne, who repeated them first hand. Frome was built as an amalgamation of seven area factories, following the West India Sugar Company's (Tate and Lyle's operating name) purchase of twenty five farms during the 1930s in Jamaica. On opening, large crowds of men had gathered around the gates eager for work, but hope was soon replaced by desperation when it became clear that there were not enough jobs to go round. It was the ensuing riots that gave rise to organised labour in Jamaica. Out of the fury surrounding the factory gates, the Industrial Trade Union of Alexander Bustamante emerged (the BITU, which remains significant in the sugar sector today) to negotiate the first labour contract the next year. Following this, the National Workers Union (NWU) under the leadership of Norman Manley gained full bargaining rights. The Colonial Office went on to accept Bustamente and Manley as rival political leaders, as their unions spawned the Jamaica Labour Party (JLP) and the Peoples' National Party (PNP) which remain, until present, at the centre of the country's political process.

The depression in the islands was lifted by the Second World War, and soon afterwards the sugar industry of the British West Indies was to prosper to new heights under improved special trade arrangements with Europe. Moreover, the seeds of nationalism that had been sown on the plantations during the 1930s were to come to fruition, as Independence was eventually granted. But with nationhood came new dilemmas for the sugar industry. Did the archaic and bitter legacy of sugar cultivation have a place in the modern states of the Caribbean? Could, and indeed should, it be part of the new drive to modernisation?

The post-war Caribbean: America's 'back-yard'

Unlike Europe, America emerged from the Second World War enormously strengthened, both economically and militarily, and thus in a unique position to propagate its economic and political viewpoint around the world. As Jenny Pearce writes, the new order it would help shape would centre around its need for large export markets and unrestricted access to raw materials; the US therefore planned on the elimination of trade restrictions, the creation of international financial bodies to stabilise currencies and the establishment of international banking institutions (as described in chapters two and three).

The overseas expansion of United States capital which subsequently took place was unprecedented: its international companies became fully global giants, which as well as dominating the American economy, came to dominate far corners of the world. Within this broader scheme, the Caribbean (and Central America) remained as America's 'back-yard' – a region where over the next half century its influence would be frequently, variously and profoundly felt, and in which the Caribbean sugar industry would become inevitably embroiled.

Roosevelt had made it clear to the British during the war years that the Americans would no longer accept its colonial presence in the region; the Commonwealth Caribbean, as much as the nominally 'independent' republic islands, was strategically part of the US 'sphere of influence'. At the same time the nationalist movement was gaining momentum in the colonies, but with their energies targeted on the old colonialists, they were less concerned with the new.

This was not the case, however, in the republic islands of the Caribbean. In Cuba, Haiti and the Dominican Republic, identified as they were with the Platt Amendment and Guantanamo Bay in Cuba, with American control of customs and finances in Haiti and the Dominican Republic –

and after a period that had seen an intensification of American control – anti-colonialism re-emerged to be re-interpreted as Anti-Americanism.

From the straightforward acts of vandalism committed by the slaves on the sugar estates in the seventeenth and eighteenth centuries, to the organised activities of the Jamaican Maroons – resistance to external domination has been a central theme of Caribbean history, as long as the colonial re-creation of the region itself. Into this story stepped Fidel Castro, who in 1959 led the revolution in Cuba. For the island, it was a 'popular' revolution, against social injustice, American control and the dominance of the sugar industry. For the region as a whole it was a political earthquake that brought the ground level manoeuvrings of the Cold War into its midst; and indeed, for a brief but terrifying moment in the annals of political history, brought the world to the brink of nuclear war.

Fidel's Cuba: sugar and the struggle of resistance

It is no accident that revolution came to the island in the modern Caribbean where the sugar industry had held the fiercest grip.

Fidel Castro was born on a West Indian sugar plantation, the son of an immigrant farm labourer from Spain who had become a prosperous landowner. As Jack Watson writes, first and foremost, Castro is a West Indian; for better or for worse, his intention was to develop a new independence and a new kind of society in and around the Caribbean. His enemies branded him, simply, as a communist, but Castroism was a West Indian product and his political persuasions differed in a variety of ways from the communism of the Soviet Union or China. Sugar was to play a pivotal role to the reform programme, as Castro firstly fought its domination of the Cuban economy and then, quickly, reconciled to embrace it.

The US-sponsored dictator Fulgencio Batista had left a legacy of corruption in Cuba. The island was in every sense an American colony and Havana a playground of casinos, highlife and mafiosi. Whatever other views he held, Castro was violently anti-American. Castroism had its origins in an intense desire to rid Cuba of foreign influences and to befriend the poor; it was a rallying cry for anti-imperialism throughout the Caribbean.

A huge gap existed in the living standards between the rich and the poor in Cuba and the mass of the island's population lived in desperate poverty with the expected accompaniments of poor housing, malnutrition and illiteracy. The island's economy was the extreme of the Caribbean

Ox-carts transporting sugar cane, Cuba   Rolando Pujol/South American Pictures

model: totally dependent on sugar, which accounted for nearly 90% of Cuba's exports, and 33% of the country's national income. American capital controlled about 75% of Cuba's arable land, and its markets absorbed two-thirds of its sugar exports. Castro's reforming programme promised the distribution of unused lands, faster industrialisation, the preservation of political and civil liberties, and an attack on corruption and illiteracy.

In the years just preceding the revolution, Cuba's sugar exports of around five million tons annually provided almost one-third of the commodity's global exports. In 1959, almost 60% of Cuba's sugar exports went to the US, then the world's largest importer, and accounted for about one-third of US domestic consumption requirements. Castro's first instinct was to attack both the overall dominance of the sugar industry and its foreign ownership. Pledging diversification, principally through a programme of accelerated industrial development, Castro reduced both the cane acreage and yield during the first few years of the revolution. Ownership of more than 995 acres by either any individual or company was also prohibited, which induced an immediate clash with US business interests. The US government quickly responded with a cut in Cuba's sugar quota for their market.

Rapid industrialisation, however, was not successful. By the mid 1960s it seemed that Cuba would have to rely on a basically agricultural economy for some time to come; and after the infamous 'Bay of Pigs' in 1961, Castro came up against the basic economic fact that no other agricultural activity would give such immediate returns as those yielded by the cultivation of sugar cane. Indeed, after Castro's tour of the Soviet Union in 1963, he had refocused; he came back with the view that 'an international division of labour' was necessary, according to which Cuba would specialise in that which it appeared to be best fitted for. As Hagelberg describes, in the face of rising import bills and a growing Balance of Payments deficit, Ernesto 'Che' Guevara, then Minister for Industry, concluded:

'The entire economic history of Cuba has demonstrated that no other agricultural activity would give such returns as those yielded by the cultivation of the sugar cane. At the onset of the Revolution many of us were not aware of this basic economic fact, because a fetishistic idea connected sugar with our dependence on imperialism and with the misery in the rural areas, without analysing the real causes: the relation to the unequal balance of trade.'

Castro came to rely heavily on the Communist world both for a market for its sugar and for supplies of desperately needed imports. Bonds between Cuba and the Soviet Union tightened in 1962 when Russia agreed to take on increased supply of Cuban sugar. As Pollit and Hagelburg relate, in a speech in Havana in 1964, Castro emphasised the difference between monoculture under the Americans and his own monoculture:

'The Soviet Union did not have any sugar plantations in Cuba. It did not have any sugar mills in Cuba. It did not have any property in Cuba. The Soviet Union was not receiving foreign exchange from Cuba. The Soviet Union did not collect dividends. It did not collect interest. On the contrary, the Soviet Union was extending large loans to Cuba to allow us to cope with this situation'.

The revolution that was to overthrow the sugar legacy in fact was to succeed only in intensifying it. With markets in the Soviet Union now secured, Castro announced that sugar production, which totalled less than 4 million tons in 1963, would be progressively increased until it reached 10 million tons by 1970. In reality, by 1970, a record crop of 8.5 million tons were produced. Cuban state planners realised early on that cane

Sugar refinery, Cuba   *Rolando Pujol/South American Pictures*

production techniques would have to be modernised and that the future of the industry was predicated on mechanisation of cane cutting in particular. However, the progress towards this was inevitably slow. Only 1% of the 1970 crop was successfully cut by machines; but by 1980, 45% was mechanically harvested.

By 1978 Castro's regime was beginning to make some sort of economic progress. Sugar still comprised up to three-quarters of Cuba's exports, but with Russia's help nickel production was expanding and growth rates were substantial. The rise of world sugar prices in the mid 1970s, combined with some generosity in price from the Russians, produced a healthy Balance of Payments. In the late 1980s, between 50 and 60 per cent of Cuban exports went to the Soviet Union, which had become the world's leading importer, accounting for almost 30% of Soviet domestic needs. At end of that decade, Cuba and the world's four other top exporters (as chapter two described, the European Union, Australia, Brazil and Thailand) together accounted for two-thirds of annual global exports of sugar.

As Pollit and Hagelburg summarise, in the thirty years following the Cuban revolution, Cuba's sugar production grew by 40% and its sugar exports by a third. Although its share of world output fell from around 12% to under 8%, Cuba remained the world's largest sugar exporter. As in pre-Revolutionary times, sugar was at the close of the 1980s the mainstay of Cuba's foreign trade and the principal earner of foreign exchange. Sugar cane growing and processing still constituted, after the commercial sector, the biggest branch of the Cuban economy. At the end of the 1980s the industry accounted for nearly a fifth of Cuba's industrial labour force and more than a third of all state sector farm workers. In some eyes the enduring prominence of the sugar industry in Cuba has been an anachronism that resisted radical transformation. Even ideological revolution of the most radical kind was unable to undo the legacy of the region's shared history.

The post-Revolutionary Cuban experience provides an extraordinary window on the geopolitics of sugar in the post-war period. As the island's struggle to fulfil the social commitments of the Revolution became ever more intimately linked to the success of its sugar industry, so the latter became deeply embroiled in the politics of the Cold War. Quotas and trade arrangements were the gauge of political affiliation on the global stage; commodity production, as in previous centuries, remained directly linked to hegemony and the power struggles of nation states. Cuba had been a political earthquake, and so great were the waves created by its Revolution that the sugar industries of other islands around the Caribbean Sea were also profoundly affected. As the colonial strings of previous times were being cut, new ones constrained prospects for change.

The Jamaican sugar industry in the post-war years

The post-war experience of Jamaica and its sugar industry encapsulates the economic battles shared by many newly independent states as they embraced de-colonialism. The 1960s were a period of growth, optimism and some degree of diversification; the 1970s were characterised by a drive towards self-determination, social redistribution and an attempt to achieve a stronger positioning in the international economy; and the 1980s, by capitulation to the international debt financiers and the attendant restrictions and social costs of structural adjustment. In Jamaica the sugar industry offered a window on these processes. In the 1960s, emphasis was placed on other forms of economic activity, even as the sugar industry recovered from its pre-war low; in the 1970s, it was a central focus of struggles against the 'neo-colonial' force of multinational penetration and the site of experimentation with co-operative working practices. In the 1980s, the World Bank and IMF became conditioning agents of its direction.

After the Second World War, it was a mass nationalist movement, grown up from the trade unions of the sugar industry and the emergence of political parties, which demanded ministerial government, self-government, and independence in rapid succession. By the end of 1966, Britain had granted complete independence to Jamaica, and also to Trinidad and Tobago, Guyana and Barbados. Colonialism, however, had left the islands with few options for their future. Bauxite, oil and tourism became the economic spearhead of the United State's penetration of the Commonwealth Caribbean. The mining of bauxite was controlled by some six multinationals, while real expansion in American tourism in the Caribbean occurred in the 1960s, following the demise of Cuba as the playground of the rich.

Following the conventional wisdom of economic theory in the 1960s, Jamaica adopted an Import Substituting Industrialisation strategy in the form of a highly protectionist trade regime, using tariffs, quantitative restrictions and an overvalued exchange rate to protect an inefficient, capital-intensive and monopolistic manufacturing industry. Bustamente introduced five-year development planning. Industrial expansion was promoted by the Jamaica Industrial Development Corporation, and bauxite, clothing manufacture, oil-refining and cement-making contributed to Jamaica's growth. Agriculture continued to make a vital contribution too, and the encouragement of tourism helped to increase the island's earnings.

But it was not easy to pay for imports and a growing population hampered the spread of prosperity. For a time, emigration to Britain helped to ease the pressure, until Britain imposed immigration restrictions in the 1960s. By the 1970s Jamaica was still struggling to provide full employment, to conquer illiteracy and to balance its books; along with unmet expectations came disillusionment, crime, industrial unrest, political gang warfare, inflation and fluctuating prices for sugar and bauxite.

As has been described above, the sugar industry had almost disappeared from Jamaica in the first part of the twentieth century. It was not until the penetration of multinational corporations between 1930 and 1945 that average factory output increased substantially. By the 1940s, the industry had regained its premier position among the island's exports, and Tate and Lyle, moreover, had established itself as its dominant force. The subsequent signing of the Commonwealth Sugar Agreement (CSA) with Britain in 1951, which provided a regular outlet for fixed quantities of sugar and assured Jamaica of continued access to the British market, propelled the industry, under the dominance of foreign capital, into great growth in the post-war period. Protected from the world market by the special trade agreement, the companies expanded operations and production increased dramatically. Between the early 1940s and early 1960s, exports increased at an average annual rate of around 10%, while revenues from sugar sales increased at the phenomenal rate of nearly 50%. By the 1960s, as Carl Feuer describes, almost a third of the entire cultivated area in Jamaica, and a much higher percentage of the best arable land, was devoted to cane production.

However, under the protection of the guaranteed market provided by the colonial power, the problems of the industry that had established themselves many years before, and had made it unviable under world market conditions, were reinforced. Most of the growth that had occurred had been based, in the quest for increased factory throughput, on increased inputs of progressively more marginal land rather than improvements in efficiency. Productivity had not actually increased significantly after 1940. Cane quality had deteriorated from the 1950s; sugar recovery rates had failed to improve; and estate production costs, starting in 1950, had escalated rapidly. By international standards, Jamaican factories were too small in terms of grinding capacity; a lack of capital investment in machinery accelerated a trend toward technological deterioration; yields of cane quality indices fell alarmingly; and factory non-performance reached crisis proportions. Production was highly labour intensive, with a requirement of nearly three times as many person hours to produce a ton of sugar than a comparable US factory. Jamaica had become the highest cost cane producer in the Commonwealth, and possibly the world.

Meanwhile, although the industry's revenues had risen at an unparalleled rate after the signing of the CSA, commissions which were publicly appointed to investigate the industry highlighted grave problems. The Goldenburg Commission (1960) noted the stark contrast of the living standards of its workers, which continued to reflect a background of poverty, underemployment and seasonal unemployment. The industry's expansion had done nothing to improve the notoriously poor socio-economic circumstances associated with its employment. For both economic and social reasons, then, the industry's trajectory of recovery proved unsustainable. From 1965 onwards, the estates recorded financial deficits each year, and before the Mordecai Commission reported in 1967, a dramatic downturn in sugar production had begun.

At the time of the Mordecai enquiry, the sugar industry was the largest employer of labour in the country, contributed about 23% of the value of visible exports and occupied 25% of good arable land. Its future was described as a matter of 'grave concern' and its survival presumed to be imperative. Mordecai's recommendations for the rationalisation of the 18 factories that were at that time operating island-wide, and the introduction of mechanical harvesters were, however, ignored.

Under Michael Manley's leadership, the 1970s were pivotal years for Jamaica. As he describes in *Jamaica: Struggle in the periphery*, Manley sought to put into practice the ideas of non-aligned development that were the common currency of academics and Third World politicians at the time; he tried to embrace real independence from old and new forces of imperialism. Over the decade his stance led Jamaica into serious conflict with the United States who feared another Cuba on their doorstep; it also led to the departure of Tate and Lyle. Short-term political expediency, reinforced after 1972 by Manley's doctrine of democratic socialism, dictated that government policy was primarily concerned with the number of jobs that the industry provided. The refusal to capitulate to Tate and Lyle's demand for the introduction of mechanical harvesters was coupled with increasing losses on their estates and they could see no reason to stay.

During the 1970s, the role of the sugar industry and its future engaged both cane workers and academics alike. Manley's socialist platform led to the transferral of the largest estates to worker-run co-operatives, representing probably the most significant initiative in land reform in the island's history. At the University of the West Indies, meanwhile, theoretical ideas of 'plantation economy' were being espoused (see, for example, Beckford, 1970). This strand of political economy – linked to wider ideas of dependency theory – considered the specific plantation history of the Caribbean to be a unique feature which influenced the nature of engagement with the world economy. In its contemporary setting, the university economists viewed the diversification of the economy that had taken place – into bauxite, tourism and light manufacturing, for instance – to merely be replicating the old colonial plantation based relationships, but this time with modern multinationals.

The 'Great Sugar Debate', as it was later known, focused specifically upon the future of the sugar industry itself in Jamaica, although it raised central questions for the British West Indies as a whole. When Britain joined the European Economic Community in 1973, continued security for Caribbean sugar producers was one of the terms Britain negotiated. Amidst the concern amongst Jamaican politicians and the media that this might, however, not be achieved, the 'Great Sugar Debate' led the academics from the University of the West Indies – who became known as the *New World Group* – to pronounce that the loss of preferential trade arrangements and ultimately, the loss of the industry as a whole, would be to the long-term benefit of Jamaica.

The debate originated from a written response by Havelock Brewster, a university economist, to the then Jamaican Prime Minister, Hugh Shearer. Shearer was reported to have said (in *the Daily Gleaner*) that 'it was a matter of life or death' that his country achieve associated non-European status in the Community if Britain's bid for membership was accepted. He was also reported to have 'discarded the theories of statisticians' who he said had been 'urging him to diversify Jamaica's agriculturally- oriented economy'. *New World* issued Brewster's response in a pamphlet entitled 'The sugar industry – our life or death', where a series of arguments were put forward for severing links with the industry and thus, the island's past. Following this, Robert Kirkwood, (of the Sugar Manufacturers Association) initiated a counter attack. The *New World Group* organised a 'teach in' for 'meaningful dialogue before the bar of public opinion', from which the following extracts are taken:

> Brewster: 'The strongest alternative, I think, is that the sugar industry should be completely abandoned at once. We should be thankful if others do it for us. The logic of this approach is to create such extreme conditions that of necessity we would find, rather quickly, what the alternatives are. In the course of finding these a new type of social, economic and political organisation would, by the very nature of the problem, become necessary.'

> Kirkwood's response:' I'll tell you what the alternatives are – a tremendous reduction in the standard of living of the people of Jamaica... and the destitution in many of the country parishes... I venture to prophesy that far from being a dying industry, West Indian farmers will be growing cane in preference to other more difficult and less easily marketable crops, long after even the youngest

member, the children I say, amongst our audience has passed on. That's my prophecy'.

As we know, the special trade arrangement was maintained as the Sugar Protocol was born. Thirty years later, the same debates are being pursued – albeit with less energy and a sense of inevitability – once again in Jamaica.

In an attempt to make radical improvements in housing, Michael Manley imported prefabricated units from Cuba in the mid 1970s. By this time his party, the PNP, had moved to the left and forged a variety of links with Castro. In contrast, Edward Seaga, who took over the leadership of the JLP from Shearer, advocated closer ties with the US and a stronger emphasis on private enterprise. There appeared to be genuine choice in 1976 election – although Manley was forced to introduce a state of emergency with a special Gun Court to deal with a growing wave of political violence. Manley won an impressive vote of confidence and apparent widespread approval of his party's drive towards socialism. Castro visited Jamaica in 1977, and Manley's government took steps towards taking control of the Reynold Jamaica Mines which extracted the island's bauxite, and the island's banks. The movement had begun amongst intellectuals, but in the 1970s it was making headway amongst voters.

However, seeds of doubt in the efficacy of Manley's programme were already sprouting. Within the sugar industry, the co-operative scheme, which had inherited an industry which was already in serious decline, lasted for only six years during which sugar production in Jamaica fell by a third as the volume of exports was halved. Despite a guaranteed market and a preferential price in Europe, and an additional quota from the United States, only twelve factory farms remained in operation in 1978. As the national economy became increasingly indebted, the industry survived on government finance alone.

The First World Bank Rehabilitation Project, which began in 1978, may be perhaps viewed as a final turning point in the modern history of the crop's production in Jamaica. As had been the case before, it was a window on change in the wider political economy of the island, as Manley lost power. As the island became one of the most heavily indebted countries in the world, and its government went into *de facto* receivership to the multilateral lending agencies, a series of development loans were used in an attempt to improve the performance of the three largest remaining estates – Frome, Monymusk and Bernard Lodge – under the doctrine of structural adjustment. After peak production levels of over 500,000 tons in the 1960s, production from the mid 1980s hovered at a little over 200,000 tons per year.

As Jane Harrigan writes, it is tempting to blame the economic crisis of the late 1970s largely on the expansionist fiscal policies of Manley's PNP in 1972-80. But the seeds of crisis were sown in the development strategy of the 1960s, after which a series of shocks in the 1970s – the oil price crisis and the collapse of export prices – exposed the fragility of early success of post-independence strategy. Most telling though, was the island's inability to shake off the legacy of the past. The industry remained, to lurch from crisis to crisis, never able to throw off its associations with poverty and rural hopelessness. And importantly, so too did the nature of unequal trading relationships that the sugar industry had established.

Slaughter, slavery and the sugar industry in the Dominican Republic

As the United States severed its links with the Cuban sugar industry after its revolution, so it strengthened those with the Dominican Republic. In 1960, as the Cuban sugar quota was suspended, the Dominican Republic became one of the chief suppliers to the US market. The American market, conversely, became the principle recipient of Dominican sugar, taking on average over 80% of total Dominican shipments. Indeed, throughout the post-War period, the country's sugar industry – a mixture of publicly and privately owned enterprise – has remained dependent on this relationship with the United States. For the US, of course, the commodity trade was based as much upon the need to secure political hegemony as sugar supplies – and, at times, this latter aim required more than a trade relationship. When, for instance, in 1965, the political situation on the island appeared to offer the potential for another communist country to emerge in the 'American Mediterranean', US troops invaded to 'restore peace'. But even as political power shifted in the island, sugar and political allegiance remained intimately linked, as the dependence upon the American consumer was deepened.

It is not just this special trade relationship with the United States that the Dominican sugar industry has relied upon. It has also been dependent upon Haitian immigration to labour in the cane fields. This relationship is something altogether of a different nature than the intra-island 'swallow' migrations that have been described earlier, or the seasonal migration between Jamaican sugar estates described in chapter one. As the Dominican Republic made economic progress in the post-war period, allowing diversification – as with other Caribbean islands – into bauxite and tourism, its sugar industry remained based around a labour situation akin to slavery. While its revenues from the cane fields were secured and inflated by its preferential treatment from the States, Haitian labourers were subject to treatment of such inhumanity as to attract international outcry, and to place the conditions of poverty and hardship described in Gaythorne in chapter one, for instance, in pale comparison. So notable is this obscene feature of its industry that it is worth some focus here.

The abuse of the human rights of Haitian labourers has its antecedents in the pre-war period in the Dominican Republic, when Rafael Trujillo became the effective ruler of the island in 1930. In 1937 he ordered the massacre of the Haitian population and was responsible for the deaths of between 15,000 and 20,000 Haitians. As Roger Plant has documented, in 1942 the government of Haiti enacted laws to stem the clandestine traffic of Haitians to the Dominican Republic, but under Trujillo, and with American investment, the latter's sugar industry expanded and so did the need for labour.

In 1948, and building on the pre-war developments in the nation's sugar industry, Trujillo constructed his first sugar mill, and in 1951, the first bilateral agreement was drawn up between Trujillo and the Haitian dictator 'Papa Doc', for the import of Haitian *braceros* (labourers). Ingenio Haina, built by Trujillo and claimed by him to be the world's largest sugar mill, came into production, and between 1955 and 1960 sugar production increased from 600,000 to over a million tons.

In 1959, before Trujillo's assassination, the bilateral agreement was renewed. With his death, however, came the nationalisation of the twelve sugar mills that were now in operation, and under Juan Bosch, a pronouncement of the onset of a programme of 'land and dignity' – promising to reduce dependence on sugar and attack corruption. By 1965 production was 500,000 tons less than five years previously. Bosch, however, was too radical for the army and charged with being a communist. He was overthrown by a military coup and Civil War instigated the arrival of US forces.

New elections led to Joaquín Balaguer, an authoritarian anti-socialist becoming President. There was no more emphasis on getting rid of the sugar industry and production quickly rose again. At the same time, there was some progress to diversification. During the next ten years, benefiting from active government, the Dominican Republic began to make progress. Although still primarily agricultural, the economy was helped by the working of bauxite and the encouragement of tourism.

No progress was made however, on the conditions in the cane fields. The bilateral contract was renegotiated in 1966 after the succession of Joaquín Balaguer, and between 1966 and 1978 a price of 60 Dominican pesos (then worth US $60) was paid to 'Papa Doc' and then to 'Baby Doc' Duvalier by the Dominican government, for each Haitian worker supplied for the sugar harvest. Despite some instability in the 1960s, production in the 1970s surged to over one million tons.

Anti-Slavery International has undertaken detailed research into the unending plight on Haitian labourers since the first international outcries in the 1970s. With the fall of the Duvalier dynasty came widespread Haitian opposition to the recruitment of Haitian *braceros* for the sugar harvest. But, as they report, the ensuing shortage of workers, the collapse in world sugar prices of the early 1980s and the continuing mismanagement and corruption in the sugar industry caused the Dominican authorities to continue and expand their coercive labour practices by forcing more Haitians living in the Dominican Republic to cut sugar cane. In the 1980s, *Anti Slavery International* estimated that up to 15,000 Haitians were forcibly recruited from Haiti and the Dominican Republic and compelled to work:

> The Dominican State Sugar Authority (CEA)... employs over 40,000 Haitians (90 per cent of the total workforce) to do the work that few Dominicans are willing to do. Private sugar estates also employ a predominantly Haitian workforce but conditions are reputed to be better on these than on the state-controlled plantations.
>
> ...Among the perennial complaints made against the Dominican authorities is the refusal of the Dominican government to provide adequate immigration documentation to Haitian migrant workers and the denial of citizenship rights to those born in the Dominican Republic of Haitian parents... These rejections of the rights of Haitians are more unacceptable when seen in the context of the Dominican government's policy of actively encouraging or forcing many Haitians to cross the border into the Dominican Republic in order to cut sugar cane... A conservatively estimated 500,000

Haitians live permanently but illegally in the Dominican Republic. Many of these are cane cutters and their families who have settled after working for the sugar harvest...

In the bateyes, or plantation work camps, there has traditionally been little schooling, few facilities and almost no health care... The camps are closed and patrolled by armed guards: no one is allowed out; visitors are not permitted... Kongos, or new recruits, sleep up to eight to a room on steel beds with no mattresses. Cane cutters are often stripped of their clothes and belongings to prevent them from escaping, while they continue to work up to 14-hour days. Latrines are few and running water is a tap shared by many people. Until recently, workers were paid in vouchers accepted only at the company stores, keeping the Haitians tied to the plantation... While thousands of Haitians are forced to cut sugar cane, many thousands more come to work on the plantations voluntarily, pushed by the terrible poverty of their own country – for although the Dominican Republic is poor, Haiti is poorer still.

During the 1970s and the early 1980s, Dominican sugar production grew largely because of high guaranteed US quotas, and continued to play a major role in the economy. It was the largest source of the country's foreign exchange earnings, and accounted for about 10% of total cultivated land. In 1983, the Dominican Republic produced a peak production of 1.2 million tons of sugar – with exports of that commodity accounting for 35% of the country's foreign exchange earnings. By 1989, however, the production level had fallen to 800,000 tons, yielding only 19 per cent of export earnings.

As with Cuba, the Dominican Republic does not have access to trade with the EU under the sugar protocol, although it has received aid through Lomé according to its definition as a country requiring special assistance. In light of this, and its continued support by the US sugar regime, it is hard to believe that over 200 years since the first successful slave revolt on the Caribbean island now shared by Haiti and the Dominican Republic, men, women and children continue to labour under conditions akin to slavery in its sugar industry.

Table 6
Sugar production 1950-1999 in thousands of metric tonnes

	1950	1960	1970	1980	1990	1999
Barbados	191,000	156,000	160,000	135,000	70,000	53,205
Cuba	5,759,000	5,862,000	7,559,000	6,805,000	8,445,000	3,874,931
Dominican Republic	532,000	1,112,000	1,014,000	1,013,000	590,000	420,909
Haiti	58,000	60,000	66,000	65,000	35,000	10,000
Jamaica	272,000	431,000	382,000	236,000	209,000	211,540
St Kitts/Nevis	-	0	33,000	36,000	25,000	20,000
Trinidad & Tobago	-	221,000	222,000	114,000	122,000	91,760

Source: International Sugar Organisation, 2000

Barbados: a lasting plantocracy

Barbados, the first jewel in the crown in the fledging era of the colonial sugar industry, presents yet another perspective on the post-war challenge left by the historical legacy of cane cultivation. As with other islands in the British West Indies, rural stagnation, out-migration and a desperate need for diversification are common themes. Its uniqueness, however, lies in the retention of a 'plantocracy' long after the ownership of the sugar industry in other islands had been centralised. Moreover, the decline in the fortunes of its sugar industry over the last two decades is probably the most obviously terminal of the islands discussed here.

In 1966, at the time of independence, Barbados had a competent civil service, a respected judiciary and a comparatively well-developed educational system, judged by standards elsewhere in the West Indies. In the Caribbean context, incomes and living standards were relatively high on the island. Its problem – typically – was the domination of the economy by sugar. More than half of the cultivated land was given over to cane, and Barbados had little else to export.

Throughout the post-independence period, however, and with the aid of government development plans, the sugar industry became progressively less significant as tourism and manufacturing expanded. Without minerals, the island forced a role for itself as a significant exporter of manufacturing, and most importantly, became a site of large-scale tourism. But despite such rapid growth, Barbados consistently experienced significant deficits in its trade balance and sank heavily into debt.

Sugar covered as much as 20,000 hectares in the 1960s. Production stood at 50,000 tons in the first decade of the century; it tripled in the period up to 1970, peaking at a record high level of over 200,000 tons in 1967. Like Jamaica, Barbados had access to British markets under the Commonwealth Sugar Agreement, and subsequently to European markets through Lomé. Following a period of high returns during the 1960s, sugar was still seen as being highly significant and quite viable. But production declined by over 60 per cent between 1967 and 1980, and fell by another third during the 1980s, as the acreage under cultivation dwindled by a third. As output dropped to around 50,000 tons, it was unable to meet both domestic demand and the EU quota. By the end of the 1980s, cane production had fallen to nineteenth century levels and the industry was on the point of total collapse.

143

Several interrelated factors have been proposed for the industry's dismal decline. Rising domestic wage costs, as diversification offered better opportunities elsewhere, were key; as was the rapid decline in numbers in estate workers. Farm management practices were as inefficient as those in Jamaica, with consequent declining yields. The islands' small size, even amongst Caribbean islands, was probably a contributory factor, making it more difficult to instigate efficiencies through economies of scale. But equally significant was the pattern of social relations and property rights which persisted from the island's colonial past. Some 100 plantations remain the principle cane producers in Barbados (with an additional 10,000 small-holders harvesting very small amounts of cane on a part time basis). An influential elite group have been able to effectively sustain their individual interests irrespective of the consequences for the sugar sector.

What is unique about Barbados is the extent to which the archaic pre-emancipation plantation system had survived almost intact during the radical change of the nineteenth century that had gone on in all the other major sugar islands (described in the previous chapter). The white minority still controlled most of the sugar sector, and the social status conferred by the ownership of an estate was far more important than purely economic considerations. Barbados was the only Commonwealth Caribbean sugar exporter whose private sector controlled the sugar industry, but there was an apparent lack of commitment to the industry itself and instead, a greater flexibility and entrepreneurship for new enterprises outside of it.

As Michael Allen writes, the concentration and corporatisation of the plantation sector that took place elsewhere in the nineteenth century did not get under way in Barbados until well into the twentieth century. Moreover, when it did happen in the early decades of century, it did not follow the patterns of other islands – rather than involving the participation of metropolitan-based mercantile houses, it instead revolved around the penetration of a locally-based commercial sector.

White plantation society in Barbados has been extremely fluid and highly stratified internally – throughout the twentieth century estate and factory ownership have been extremely diverse. Alongside what Allen refers to as an agribusiness bourgeoisie are other types of owners: some established local and absentee proprietors who had weathered the depression years of the late nineteenth century, as well as various groups originating from a poor white or poor yeomanry stock who had acquired capital to buy into estates. Absentee ownership, however, remained a prominent feature. The

Kendal Estate, St John's, Barbados, c1920s　　　　　　　*Picture courtesy of John Gilmore*

attorney system – a legacy of the days of foreign absentee ownership – constitutes the central element of the management structure. An attorney represents the interests of the absentee owners of an estate, although often they manage more than one; under him there is a manager responsible for the day-to-day management activities.

Important links were forged between the commercial bourgeoisie and the planter class as early as 1920 – in particular, the relationship between the plantocracy and the two Barbadian agri-business conglomerates, Barbados Shipping and Trading, and Plantations Limited, have been of great importance. Private plantation corporations have inter-locked directorships with the two giants and significant ownership of shares. This diversification of financial interests is a process which continued into the 1960s and 1970s, in what was considered by the planter elite to be a safe investment, able to generate an income to offset any losses that may occur in agriculture. Increasing overheads and decreasing revenues from sugar resulted in a situation of loss for many estate owners. As well as some divestment and diversification of estate land, they diversified their economic interests – independently and via the two conglomerates – into tourism, commerce and agribusiness. The plantocracy did not need to keep their eyes firmly on sugar – instead, they were juggling more interesting and profitable balls.

145

In the 1960 and 70s, 120 estates went completely out of sugar production. Amidst this fragmentation, land remained far too expensive for small-farmers, but the middle classes purchased it for the building of private homes. Much of the remainder was abandoned to return to bush. Some of the elite also emigrated, with absentee ownership remaining as a prominent feature. But although earnings from sugar exports fell dramatically, they remained one of very few sources of foreign exchange, and the Barbadian government embarked on a massive programme of support during the 1980s, furnished largely by the Barbados National Bank.

Publicly owned plantations have been in distinct minority in Barbados. But semi-public ownership of indebted factories and plantations have provided the basis for the co-operation with the government. In 1992, similarly to Jamaica, tenders were invited from firms wishing to plan and manage a restructuring of the Barbados sugar industry. Again, as with Jamaica, Booker Tate – a jointly owned subsidiary of Tate and Lyle and Booker plc – came in, to control both strategic planning and day to day management. But the decline has been inexorable – and without the Sugar Protocol, it is difficult to imagine any future at all for the island's sugar industry.

A century of struggle

The first chapters of this book have outlined the nature of the crisis that the sugar islands of the Caribbean face. The outlook is bleak because of a series of inter-related factors: the doubtful future of the Sugar Protocol (which grew out of the Lomé Convention), the reform of the Common Agricultural Policy, the uncertainties of the US sugar programme, and competition from artificial sweeteners. Moreover, the nature of the world market for sugar, together with the workings of transnational business, create further inequities in the international commodity trade. In addition to this, Cuba has faced an increasingly hostile external environment since the collapse of Comecon and the disintegration of the Soviet Union, which has demolished the certainties on which the country's economic development strategy was based. Throughout the twentieth century, geopolitics have played a key role in dictating the fortunes of cane cultivation in the region. Now, the geopolitics of the post-Cold War era, and the region's relative insignificance within them, appear to herald its collapse. The sugar industries of the Caribbean are in a turmoil from which they will not emerge without undergoing drastic adjustments.

Against the backdrop of external forces, local circumstances have also contributed to the continued decline in the industry's performance. During the 1990s, as the table shows, the declines that began in earlier decades have continued. There are, of course, very different internal circumstances on each island – in size, in the structure of their economies, and in the nature of their dependence upon sugar – but at the same time they share many common problems with their neighbours. Each nation in the Caribbean region is unique, and it would be foolish to over-emphasise either their current similarities or the nature of the problems that their sugar industries face – but similarities arise both from their common heritage during centuries of King Sugar, and in the battles that they have fought in their attempts to overcome it.

The failure to manage extensive economic diversification has led, in the final decades of the century, to the common experience of debt, which earlier chapters have addressed. This has been intensified both by commodity dependence and by the lingering plantation/small farm conflict in rural areas. As we saw in chapter one, the lack of domestic agriculture has led to a food deficit situation, placing further stress on Balance of Payments. Rural outmigration is another common theme. Within the sugar industry itself, mechanisation has remained a problem for all islands – because of terrain, because of lack of investment, and because of the critical need for jobs. Poor plant husbandry, an historic lack of investment in factory and field, and the continuing socio-cultural connotations of the past have all contributed to the industry's decline. Most importantly, the relationship between employment in the cane fields and desperate poverty in the home has never been broken.

The experiences of the twentieth century have illustrated the tenacious grip of the sugar legacy in Jamaica and the wider Caribbean. Clearly, its economic importance has faded, and in a social sense it has become an irrelevance to those living beyond the rural plantations. But equally its collapse would not be without severe casualties. Chapters four and five have presented a Caribbean view of the sugar industry – of the common history of a region recreated, in the colonial era, for the purpose of cultivating cane. Now we return to our focus of Jamaica, and the village of Gaythorne, and consider the future for those who are living and working on a present-day plantation.

Chapter Six

Bitter Future? Prospects for Change

'The social fabric of cane growing and production is something that is 200 years old. To change it is the only long-term solution. But the pain of changing it, on top of everything else that is going on, is something that in the short term is disastrous...' Jamaican plantation manager

Along the main tarmacked road that runs through Gaythorne, a small group of young guys in their late teens and twenties sit together under the shade of trees. They congregate in the early afternoon and they'll stay put for several hours – drinking a coke or beer, smoking cigarettes or perhaps ganja. They salute the people they know who pass by on foot, donkey or in vehicles, and stare curiously at those they do not recognise. They are dressed smartly – fashionable trousers, t-shirts embossed with logos, the obligatory dark shades. These 'frontliners' as they are known, observe cane farmers and manual labourers walk past in ragged work clothes, swinging a machete and other tools as they make their way to their cane fields or farm plots. They watch the open top bus from the local Long Pond sugar estate transporting the field workers from Gaythorne to the fields. And they wave to the drivers of the cane trucks that rattle along the tarmac, shedding sticks of cane from their load as they go.'

The frontliners are greeted by the young women who pass; other young guys stop for a chat. But they rarely get approached by the farmers who are offering day labouring jobs or others who may be looking for someone to help them with manual work for a few hours. Everybody in Gaythorne knows that the guys at the side of the road are waiting for something to happen: to be 'picked up' by the local 'big men', to be offered a chance for 'fast' ways to make money. They are not interested in 'dirty' work. They're dressed for 'hussling' tourists or doing a 'deal' – and they are not strangers to the more illicit aspects of the local economy. For certain, they have rejected the sugar economy and its connotations, and the type

Cutting cane sugar by hand, Cuba   *Rolando Pujol/South American Pictures*

of work forced upon their parents and grandparents' generations through economic necessity. Their own horizons are with the big hotels on the coast, the fast cars driven by the successful husslers, and most importantly, foreign shores.

The guys on the frontline are the pioneers of a generation in Gaythorne who are trying to abandon the sugar industry and its struggles – but instead, they are embracing new ones. Often criticised by their grandparents for their unwillingness to 'dirty up dem pretty shoes', and by their parents for their propensity to get themselves into trouble, they are nevertheless supported economically by their families. Indeed, more than anything, their parents want their children to be free of the hard manual labours that they have to endure. But, as chapter one explored, there are so few viable alternatives available beyond the sugar industry that it is a long and difficult battle to forge an independent means of existence. Illicit activity is hardly that when so few other opportunities are available. More reasonably, it is the obvious choice for those who are bold enough to risk its possible consequences.

Of course, although the frontliners may have rejected work for themselves in the sugar industry, they are supported by the labours of others who have not. The sugar industry is the most important source of

149

locally-generated income for the community of Gaythorne: the parents and grandparents who put the food in the 'pot' are sustained, at least in part, by their work through the sugar estate. The home in which they live, even the clothes that they are wearing, are likely to have been bought with money earned over time from labouring in the fields or factory. Despite the grinding poverty, generations of people from Gaythorne have somehow been raised and sent to school on the proceeds of employment in the sugar industry.

Without the sugar industry the frontliners themselves would not be able to sit by the road side waiting for something better to come along. Indeed, it may well be the case that with the frustrations of passing time and increasing domestic responsibilities, they will actually be forced themselves to give up their ambitions and to seek employment at the estate. If it still is in operation, that is. For, as a result of the local, national and international drivers that the book has explored, the future of Long Pond is bleak. Clearly, the impact of its closure would be profound. Not only are there few other alternatives for employment, but for generations the cyclical pattern of the sugar harvest has driven the local economy as a whole, sustaining shops, dressmakers, builders, mechanics and a whole range of small businesses.

This short concluding chapter considers the local level prospects for the sugar-growing areas of Jamaica in the first decades of the next century. It begins with a return visit to the community where the book began – with the focus that Gaythorne offers providing insights that are relevant to the island's sugar growing areas as a whole. It considers the likely path for the next decade if the sugar industry withers, and the possible local outcomes for the community. It then considers more widely the possibilities and potential that the inevitable 'roll over' period (outlined in chapter two) could offer, as the special trade relationship with Europe is renegotiated.

As chapter three described, sugar as big business has done few favours for the people of Gaythorne and Jamaica, and development initiatives for the new century must attempt to reinvent the nature of the relationship between producer and consumer. Of course, as the history of the Caribbean during recent decades has shown, small nation states are largely unable to subvert the institutionalised systems of international trade, and neither do they have the resources for autonomous development. But, perhaps there is real potential for planning that can harness new benefits from the international relationship between producer and consumer that sugar production has forged; perhaps these can be transferred to other sectors of production. In this regard, the discussion highlights some grass shoots of hope from Gaythorne that suggest pragmatic steps for the future, as well as draws to attention the urgent need for action to reduce the economic and social consequences that a future without sugar would bring.

The roots that feed the branches

'It's [the sugar industry] probably the single largest employer at the present time. You also have to consider that in addition to the estates an awful lot of the sugar is grown by cane farmers, so that you have a problem not only of the cost efficiency of the large estates, but of medium- sized cane farmers who supply maybe 40 per cent of the cane. So you're talking about unemployment for the large cane farms, a drop in price for the cane farmers – you're talking about an inability to hire labour. It has very broad implications for about 30 to 40 per cent of the rural population of Jamaica.'
Professor Donald Robotham, Vice Chancellor, University of the West Indies at Mona

'There are many reasons for the lack of mechanisation. Some in the past have been political and social. If we are to compete sufficiently and reduce our costs, in order to make sufficient money to reinvest and to improve the whole operation, both the growing and the manufacturing of sugar, then we are going to have to mechanise. And small farmers will increasingly have to be left out. To be anywhere near efficient you need to be growing at least 500 acres of cane; some of our cane farmers are growing less than an acre. In the future, the estates need to grow as much of the cane as they can, together with being supplied by very large independent farmers who have at least 500 acres. And that land must be producing at least 25 tonnes of cane per acre. Anything less is not viable, but we've got small farmers producing ten or twelve tonnes on their acre. They just can't afford the fertiliser, the labour, the outlay necessary... this can't carry on...'
Jamaican plantation manager

As chapter one explained, the circumstances at the Long Pond sugar estate have been in serious decline over the last decades. At best, and only with major capital investment and improved field and factory practices, it can survive into the first decade of the twenty first century – with the introduction of mechanical harvesters in the cane fields, and with the contributions of small (individual) cane farmers largely excluded from the workings of the estate. The worst-case scenario is that Long Pond will close and the sugar economy in the parish of Trelawny will collapse. Either way, the livelihoods of thousands of people in the parish will be affected.

In Gaythorne, both the nature of individual engagement in the sugar economy, and the form of occupational multiplicity that an individual undertakes varies according to age, gender and family situation. Although the perceived wisdom is that the workforce of the sugar industry is ageing, men and women of all ages – from school-leavers to 90 year-olds – are involved. It is certainly the case that it is the young men and women in Gaythorne who are most vociferous in their loathing of the industry, but lack of alternative means that there is nonetheless a long informal 'waiting list' of school-leavers hoping for the chance of a job in the sugar factory. Moreover, whereas the sugar industry is associated with poverty and lack of choice, it also contributes to the incomes of relatively wealthy households as well as those of the poorest. As chapter one illustrated, some households in Gaythorne have made money from working overseas and have been able, on their return, to invest in substantial cane plots and hire labour to tend to them for them; or buy trucks to transport the canes of other farmers to the factory. The loss of the industry then, would have an impact across generations and on the relatively well off as well as the poorest – and on the informal hired labour sub-economy as well.

Occupational multiplicity – the normal practice in rural Jamaica whereby people do several jobs, usually on a part time or intermittent basis – is a necessary survival strategy in a stagnant economy. As chapter one described, in Gaythorne the patterns of this illustrate the range and the limitations of other sources of available support. Most commonly, households combine their work in the sugar industry with small farming, and remittances from Kingston and overseas are very vital too. There are also a range of other activities, often self-employed, where people with skills work, for example, as mechanics or dressmakers. A few others find formal employment in the hotels on the coast or in the shops in Falmouth or Montego Bay. Generally, however, the more esteemed employment in

Stacking cane on a trailer, Cuba   *Rolando Pujol/South American Pictures*

the trade or service sectors is the hardest to come by. Many would-be mechanics, builders and taxi drivers actually spend much of the year farming their domestic plots and tending their canes.

In the short term at least, the contraction of the sugar industry is likely to make it even more difficult to find other types of work. As the major source of revenue in the local economy disappears, the knock-on effect into other sectors of activity will inevitably cause them to contract too. Reliance upon remittances will intensify, as will the desire for out-migration, to Kingston or overseas. Pressure on domestic farming plots will be increased as people are forced to expand their levels of self-sufficiency.

The shrinkage of the sugar sector, however, can not necessarily be presumed to lead to increased buoyancy in the domestic agricultural sector. The bias towards export agriculture has meant that domestic farming has traditionally been forced onto the poor soils of the steep slopes, while cane has dominated the best lowlands and received the majority of capital investment in the form of inputs. Even if the sugar industry withers, it is highly unlikely that the best lands will become available to small farmers, even if they were able to afford to buy it. It is far more likely (as with

153

Barbados, described in the previous chapter) that the cane lands would revert to bush as environmental damage on the marginal lands increased. Moreover, this timeless conflict between export (cane) and domestic (food) agriculture has led to antipathy towards small farming (or 'poor man farming' as it is often referred to by the young men in Gaythorne) in general. The inhabitants of Gaythorne are sophisticated and international in outlook; there is no room for romantic notions of a self-sufficient 'peasantry' developing in the wake of the contraction of the sugar sector.

Local people report that without Long Pond, the area would be '*dead out*', and that it would not '*be safe to walk in the road*'. With the contraction in formal and legal means of employment, and with an increase in real economic hardship, it would also only be logical to presume an increase in social unrest and an expansion of illicit activity. The drugs economy would inevitably expand; likely too would the market for stolen visas and passports. This can hardly be surprising to the international institutions that dictate the direction of trade and development policy, but it could well inject another layer of contradiction into the policy conundrum. Those who are fighting the international 'drugs war' in the Caribbean and Central America are not the same group who are pushing the WTO. to renounce special trade relationships, or the EU to consider Lomé-type arrangements outdated. It would be sensible, however, to link cause and effect, and to take a holistic view of the development dilemma that is unfolding.

It is not just the sugar industry that connects the global with the local; through the tradition of migration, the community of Gaythorne itself has diverse international linkages, especially to the United States, Britain and Canada. As sugar declines, these linkages will become even more vital – both for the survival of the community *in situ* and for the opportunities they will offer to help more people escape the stagnation of rural Jamaica. The crisis of collapse can not, then, be isolated to pockets of the island, because it will have ramifications for increased social pressure in Kingston, more desperate risks being taken in air and seaports and a heightened burden on migrants to find money to send 'home'. The 'moral' arguments for special trade arrangements of the Lomé type may have been lost to the WTO during the final decade of the twentieth century, but the former colonial powers will not be exempt from the consequences of their withdrawal.

Scenarios of change at the international level

'...The WTO assume a world without preferential agreements. Now that is an entirely different platform from in the past. If you consider the cost of production of sugar in Jamaica is about 25/26 cents, a pound, where as world market prices are around 6 or 7 cents a pound. And you get the sense of the dimension of this problem...We have to get a transitional period. We can't simply go either into a free market, or into any pricing mechanism which is linked to the free market. So the renegotiation of the Sugar Protocol in Lomé to allow us an extended period of adjustment is absolutely vital. I think the second thing here is that the government and the private sector has to sit down and to address the adjustment problems fairly and squarely. We probably need some sort of social subsidy to manage that and this has been discussed in a preliminary sort of way, but a much more aggressive effort has to be mounted...'
Professor Donald Robotham, Vice Chancellor, University of West Indies, Mona Campus

Chapter two explored in detail the different elements of the international policy conundrum that are dictating change in the trade relationships on which Jamaica's sugar industry depends. As described earlier, the European Union's position is to get a waiver for Lomé IV to be 'rolled over' and maintained in its present form until 2005. In the spring of 2000, Lomé IV was officially replaced by a new ACP/EU Partnership Agreement (the Cotonou Agreement), although this will not be formally ratified until 2002. Lomé arrangements on trade have, however, been 'rolled over' and will be maintained in their present form until 2008. In the meantime, 'successor arrangements' which must be WTO. compatible will be drawn up. The Sugar Protocol is being negotiated separately; with regard to the negotiating mandate, it is to be maintained until 2003, but requires a WTO waiver to continue beyond 2005.

Although the Protocol will continue to guarantee a market for ACP sugar over the next few years, it will not guarantee a price. The Common Agricultural Policy is itself being renegotiated, with the presumption being that this will result in a reduction in price paid to European, and hence Caribbean, farmers. So although the arrangements under the Protocol may be maintained for a few more years yet, the value of the arrangement

155

is likely to steadily decrease until the Protocol itself becomes an irrelevance to Caribbean producers. As has been explained, the conditions of sugar production at the local level in Jamaica are such that it is unable to compete competitively without a guaranteed inflated price, and thus the devaluation of the Protocol – after decades of support from Britain and then Europe – will be critical.

In Britain, the Department for International Development Select Committee on International Development (DFID) consider the renegotiation to be an opportunity for the European Union as a whole to re-examine its development priorities for the ACP countries. Ten per cent of DFID expenditure in 1998-99 will be through the Lomé Convention – therefore, as it states, it has an obligation to British tax payers to ensure that such a considerable proportion of its aid budget is spent effectively and in ways consistent with its anti-poverty strategy. In their 1998 response to the Commission, they state:

'We criticise the Commission for failing to consider properly the implications for developing countries of CAP reform. The Commission must conduct impact assessments of CAP reform proposals for developing countries and the ACP in particular.'

The post-Lomé debate is developing. The new Partnership Agreement includes a general change in the criteria of aid allocation, with more emphasis being placed on helping those countries most in need using certain indicators – as yet, it is unclear as to which ACP countries may lose out in this. There will be a move towards non-state actor involvement with a concurrent increase in private sector involvement. The eventual phasing out of all preferential trade and the ' integration' of all ACP countries into the world economy is central. Given this final point, it is vital that the 'lag' time before the end of special trade arrangements is used effectively not just for talk, but for action to plan new local strategies for job creation, to develop new ways of integrating in the global economy, and to negotiate new sources of finance to enable local level development initiatives to be implemented. As David Jessop from Caribbean Council for Europe has written, this time must be created in which:

'new industries can be developed, the service sector strengthened, competitiveness enhanced and the private sector made ready for the full force of globalisation... The European Union's development assistance should principally be targeted in ways that help ACP states integrate into the global economy, improve competitiveness, develop strong and independent private sectors, reduce poverty and integrate marginalised groups into society. In other words, the present emphasis on infrastructural programmes may give way to aid aimed at providing support for education, training, rural poverty alleviation and the creation of a new economic environment.'

If it is to be effective, the post Lomé arrangement will create new partners in co-operation. In addition to providing assistance to governments, Non-Governmental Organisations, ACP civil society and the private sector will all be instrumental in working through the development dilemmas that the Caribbean faces. History has illustrated the immense difficulties that the sugar legacy presents; there are no easy answers and certainly no blueprints for action. NGOs will continue to have an important role; new forms of partnership with the private sector must attempt to overcome the social inequities that transnational business have helped to perpetuate. Most importantly, though, development initiatives must be real and self-sustaining. The sugar industry has survived on special trade arrangements that will not exist in the twenty-first century. And whereas charity and social policy initiatives will be imperative to ameliorate the immediate and worst consequences of adjustment to the post-sugar era, the inhabitants of Gaythorne and countless other poor communities in the rural Caribbean want the chance of productive employment in sectors with a real stake in the next century. Overcoming the sugar legacy means looking to the future, and examining the potential of new modes of doing business in the world economy.

Producer and consumer – new relationships for the new era

'We have to find alternatives to the commodity markets that not only bring traders and producers together without eliminating freedom of choice, but also bring the final consumer more closely into touch with the producers themselves.'
Michael Barrat Brown, Fair Trade

'Small local firms and niche products is a key area, and of particular importance to the UK market, where there is the ethical consumer movement which has made some small but significant impact on peoples' consumption patterns. But the linkages need to be made,

157

and this is the difficulty. I think people in the Caribbean are not sufficiently aware of these opportunities and what is required to exploit them...We need a mutual learning process to take place, whereby we can develop new kinds of economic activities which are mutually beneficial to the British consumer as well as to our people...'
Professor Donald Robotham, Vice Chancellor, University of the West Indies

In the post-Lomé era, one of the most critical issues for Jamaica will be the nature of the trade relationships that it is able to develop. The sugar legacy, as chapters two and three examined, has led to trading relationships that have maintained the status quo but have failed to provide real impetus for development. Clearly, it is not an easy proposition to reinvent producer/consumer relationships, but perhaps the very connections that sugar has made – between the supermarket shelf in the developed world and the lives of those living in Gaythorne – hold one possible key to a more positive future.

Over the last decade in the UK, and elsewhere in Western Europe, there has been a rise in consumer interest in 'ethical' consumption, and fair trade. In the UK, and thanks to the activities of NGOs, 'fair traded' coffee now takes 5% of the market; meanwhile, the 'ethical' financial investment market grows year on year. The market for 'environmentally friendly' goods and organic produce is now so well developed that it can no longer be considered niche; indeed, the top British supermarkets such as Sainsbury are selling more than a million pounds worth of organic produce every week. Moreover, just as the homogenising forces of globalisation guarantee that consumers in the Western world have access to the same, ever expanding range of goods, as individuals we are becoming more and more interested in products that appear regional and authentic. Nowadays, in general, we may be putting less sugar in our tea but we are more concerned about where and how it is grown; we may be able to purchase Coca-Cola in the remotest corners of the globe, but we also want to enjoy new tastes and experiences that seem linked to geography. As consumers, we have real power to promote business activity that is of benefit to both producer and consumer – and has equitable and sustainable outcomes.

Although it may be easy, in the face of transnational business and global institutions of governance to exaggerate the potential of consumer power, nevertheless there are market opportunities available that offer openings for new forms of business. Local businesses, through the networks provided by retailers, can reach global audiences. Moreover, the movement of Jamaican people around the globe has created both market opportunities and invaluable connections. Over the last decade, small Jamaican food manufacturing businesses – including a Trelawny firm employing small numbers of people from Gaythorne – have penetrated British, American and Canadian markets with their 'traditional' sauces and condiments, selling not just to the migrant populations but 'crossing over' to the 'mainstream'. Within Jamaica, these have proved to be truly dynamic areas of the local economy – run by Jamaican people, employing Jamaican people, and sourcing much of their produce from local farmers.

Living beyond the sugar legacy

The enormous difficulties that Jamaica faces in overcoming its sugar legacy can not be underestimated. But if it can make new linkages and implement new forms of entrepreneurial activity – and face up to this departure as soon as possible – then hope lies ahead. This is true not just for the people of Gaythorne but for those across the Caribbean who have had their lives blighted, for generations, by their positioning in the international division of labour as the producers of sugar – a position that has become increasingly redundant over time. As the region adjusts to its future, mechanisms need to be created that foster the growth of new industries and entrepreneurial activity for the Caribbean – broadening the economic base through the creation of schemes that encourage small and medium size enterprise and micro enterprise. New financial mechanisms are needed, and access to long term, low interest financing. Access to Lomé resources is crucial, but it must be made available without undermining the nation states' right to determine development strategies.

All this is undoubtedly a tall order. But there is little choice unless the future is to be more blighted than the past for the sugar producing islands of the Caribbean. As we look back – over the history of exploitation, and the centuries of resistance – it is difficult to regret the collapse of the cane industry. The future undoubtedly owes those who are entwined in this bitter epoch something better. The challenge to secure it, however, is a mighty one.

Bibliography

Chapter One

Anderson, P. and Witter, M. 1991. *Crisis, adjustment and social change: a case-study of Jamaica.* United Nations Research Institute for Social Development, University of the West Indies, Kingston, Jamaica

Beckford, G. 1972. *Persistent poverty – underdevelopment in plantation economies of the third world.* Oxford University Press, republished Maroon Publishing House, Jamaica, 1988

Bluestain, H. and Le Franc, E. 1987. *Strategies for organization of small farm agriculture in Jamaica.* University of the West Indies Press/Centre for International Studies Cornell University

Clarke, E. 1957. *My mother who fathered me: a study of family life in three selected communities in Jamaica.* London: Allen and Unwin

Comitas, L. 1973. 'Occupational multiplicity in rural Jamaica.' In *Work and family life: West Indian perspectives.* D Lowenthal and L Comitas (eds) 157-173. London: Anchor Books

Davies, O. 1992. *The government of Jamaica's programmes and strategies for rural development.* Planning Institute of Jamaica, United Nations Development Programme (sponsored) Round table on collaboration between the Government of Jamaica and non-governmental organisations for rural development. Planning Institute of Jamaica, Kingston, Jamaica

Department of Statistics 1983. *Census of agriculture 1978-79.* Kingston, Jamaica

Espeut, P. 1990. 'Strategies for rural development in Jamaica: a look at rural underdevelopment in Jamaica 1838-1988 providing an appreciation of the constraints to rural development and strategies for its development.' Prepared for the *National Five Year Development Plan 1990-95.* Institute of Social and Economic Research, University of the West Indies, Kingston, Jamaica

Girvan, N. (ed) 1997. *Poverty, empowerment and social development in the Caribbean.* University of the West Indies Press

Gomes, P. I. (ed) 1985. *Rural development in the Caribbean.* Heinemann (Caribbean).

Ministry of Agriculture 1998/9. *Corporate Plan.* Ministry of Agriculture, Kingston, Jamaica

Panton, D. 1993. 'Dual labour markets and unemployment in Jamaica: a modern synthesis.' *Social and Economic Studies,* 42:1, 75-118

Pastor, R. (ed) 1985. *Migration and development in the Caribbean – the unexplored connection.* Boulder: Westview Press

Planning Institute of Jamaica 1999. *Jamaica survey of living conditions.* Kingston, Jamaica

Smith, M. G. 1985. *Poverty in Jamaica.* University of the West Indies Press

Chapter Two

Abbott, G. 1990. *Sugar.* London: Routledge

Adams, N. 1993, *Worlds Apart.* London: Zed Books

Barret Brown, M. 1993, *Fair trade – reform and realities in the international trading system.* London: Zed Books

Coote, B. 1987. *The hunger crop – poverty and the sugar industry*. Oxford: Oxfam Press

Coote, B. 1992. *The trade trap – poverty and global commodity markets*. Oxford: Oxfam Press

Griesgraber, J. and Gunter, B. 1995. *Promoting development: effective global institutions for the twenty first century*. Pluto Press/Centre for Concern

Hagelberg, G. 1974. *The Caribbean sugar industries: constraints and opportunities*. New Haven, Yale University Antilles Research Programme

Hagelberg, G. and Hannah, A.C. 1994. *Instability in the sugar market - an overview*. London: International Sugar Organisation

Madely, J. 1992. *Trade and the poor – the impact of international trade on developing countries*. London: Intermediate Technology Publications

Page, S. 1994. *How developing countries trade*. ODI in association with Routledge

Radetzki, M. 1990. *A guide to primary commodities in the world economy*. Oxford: Basil Blackwell

Select Committee on International Development fourth report 2000. The renegotiation of the Lomé Convention. See http://www.parliament.the-statione

Thomas, C. Y. 1985. *Sugar threat or challenge? An assessment of the impact of technological development in the high fructose, corn syrup and sucrochemicals industries*. IDRC/ University of the West Indies Press

Thomson, R. 1987. *Green Gold: bananas and dependency in the Caribbean*. London: Latin America Bureau

Vuilleumier, S. 1996. *World outlook for high fructose syrups to the year 2000*. International Sugar Journal, Vol 98. No. 1173

Watkins, K. 1992. *Fixing the rules: north-south issues in international trade and the GATT Uruguay round*. London: Catholic Institute for International Relations

Woodward, D. 1994. 'Reform of the EU sugar regime: implications for developing country sugar exporters.' Catholic Institute for International Relations Briefing paper.

Chapter Three

Amin, S. 1997. *Capitalism in the age of globalization: the management of contemporary society*. London: Zed Books

Barret Brown, M. 1993. *Fair trade – reform and realities in the international trading system*. London: Zed Books, op.cit.

Boyd, D. 1988. 'The impact of adjustment policies on vulnerable groups: the case of Jamaica 1973-1985.' In *Adjustment with a human face* Vol II, Cornia, Jolly and Steward (ed) London: Zed Books

Chalmin, P. 1990. *The making of a sugar giant – Tate and Lyle 1859-1989*. London: Harwood Academic Publishers

Chossudovsky, M. 1997. *The globalisation of poverty: impacts of IMF and World Bank reforms*. Zed Books and Third World Network

Hugill, A. 1978. *Sugar and all that – a history of Tate and Lyle*. London: Gentry Books

Jones, H. and Sayers, H. 1963. *The story of Czarnikow*. London: Harley Publishing Co. Ltd

Korten, D. 1995. *When corporations rule the world*. UK: Earthscan Publications

Lang, T. (et al) 2001. *A modern food poverty.* (forthcoming) London: Demos

Madely, J. 1992. *Trade and the poor – the impact of international trade on developing countries.* London: Intermediate Technology Publications, op.cit.

Schuurman, F. J. (ed) 1993. *Beyond the impasse – new directions in development theory.* London and New Jersey: Zed Press

Watkins, K. 1992. *Fixing the rules: north-south issues in international trade and the GATT Uruguay round.* London: Catholic Institute for International Relations

Chapter Four

Albert, G. and Graves, A. (eds) 1984. *Crisis and change in the international sugar economy 1860-1914.* Norwich and Edinburgh: ISC Press

Beachey, R.W.1957. *The British West Indies sugar industry in the late nineteenth century.* Oxford: Basil Blackwell

Beckles, H. and Shepherd, V. 1991. *Caribbean slave society and economy: a student reader.* Jamaica: Ian Randle Publishers. London: James Curry Publishers

Beckles, H. (ed) 1996. *Inside slavery: process and legacy in the Caribbean experience.* University of the West Indies Press

Chalmin, P. 1984. 'The important trends in sugar diplomacy before 1914.' In *Crisis and change in the international sugar economy 1860-1914.* B. Albert and A. Graves (eds) Norwich and Edinburgh: ISC Press

Craton, M. 1982. *Testing the chains – resistance to slavery in the British West Indies.* London: Cornell University Press

Eisner, G. 1961. *Jamaica 1830-1930. A study in economic growth.* Manchester University Press

Galloway, J. H. 1989. *The sugarcane industry – an historical geography from its origins to 1914.* Cambridge University Press.

Hart, R. 1998. *From occupation to Independence: a short history of the peoples of the English-speaking Caribbean.* The University of the West Indies Press

Higman, B. 1976. *Slave population and economy in Jamaica 1807-1834.* Cambridge University Press

Higman, B. 1998. *Montpelier, Jamaica: a plantation community in slavery and freedom 1739-1912.* University of the West Indies Press

Hobhouse, H. 1999. *Seeds of Change.* London: Macmillan

Mintz, S. 1984. *From plantations to peasantries in the Caribbean.* Washington: The Woodrow Wilson Centre for International Scholars

Mintz, S. 1985. *Sweetness and power – the place of sugar in modern history.* London: Viking Books

Pearce, J. 1982. *Under the Eagle: US intervention in Central American and the Caribbean.* London: Latin America Bureau

Ragatz, J. 1928. *The fall of the planter class in the British Caribbean 1763-1833 – a study in social and economic history.* New York: The Century Company

Schnakenbourg, C. 1984. 'From the sugar estate to central factory: the industrial revolution in the Caribbean (1840-1905).' In *Crisis and change in the international sugar economy 1860-1914.* B. Albert and A. Graves (eds) Norwich and Edinburgh: ISC Press

Sheridan, R. 1974. *Sugar and Slavery – an economic history of the British West Indies 1623-1775*. Caribbean University Press

Watson, J. 1979. *The West Indian heritage: a history of the West Indies*. London: Cox and Wyman Ltd

Williams, E. 1994 (reprinted). *Capitalism and Slavery.*University of North Carolina Press

William, E. 1970. *From Columbus to Castro: the history of the Caribbean, 1492-1969*. London: André Deutsch

Chapter Five

Allen, M. 1979. 'Sugar and survival: the retention of economic power by white elites in Barbados and Martinique.' In Cross, M. and A. Marks (eds), *Peasants, plantations and rural communities in the Caribbean*

Americas Watch and the National Coalition for Haitian Refugees 1991. *Half measures: reform, forced labor and the Dominican sugar industry.* Americas Watch, New York

Americas Watch and the National Coalition for Haitian Refugees 1992. *A troubled year: Haitians in the Dominican Republic.* Americas Watch, New York

Anti Slavery International 1992. *The price of sugar: Haitian forced labour in the Dominican Republic.* Resource pack for Anti Slavery International London

Beckford, G. 1972. *Persistent poverty – underdevelopmenht in plantation economies of the third world.* Oxford University Press, republished Maroon Publishing House, Jamaica, 1988

Beckford, G. 1984. *The struggle for a relevant economics.* Social and Economic Studies, Vol. 33 no 1, 47-57

Beckford, G. and Witter, M. 1980. *Small garden, bitter weed: struggle and change in Jamaica.* London: Zed Press

Beckles, H. 1990. *A history of Barbados: from Amerindian settlement to nation-state.* Cambridge University Press

Brewster, H. 1967. *Sugar: our life or death?* Jamaica: New World Publishers, Pamphlet No. 4

Feuer, C. 1984. *Jamaica and the sugar worker co-operatives: the politics of reform.* Boulder: West View Press

Ferguson, J. 1992. *Dominican Republic: Beyond the Lighthouse.* London: Latin America Bureau

Gilmore, J. 1999. *Faces of the Caribbean.* London: Latin America Bureau

Girvan, N. and Jefferson, O. 1981. *Readings in the political economy of the Caribbean – a collection of reprints and articles on Caribbean political economy with suggested further reading.* Jamaica: New World

Goldenburg Commission 1960. *Report of the sugar industry enquiry commission 1959-60.* Government printer, Kingston, Jamaica

Hagelberg, G. 1974. *The Caribbean sugar industries: constraints and opportunities.* New Haven, Yale University Antilles Research Programme

Harrigan, J. 1991. 'Jamaica.' In, Mosely, P. (et al). *Aid and power: the World Bank and policy based lending* Vol 1 and 2. Routledge

Jefferson, O. 1999. *Stabilization and stagnation in the Jamaican economy 1972-1997: some reflections on macro-economic policy over the past twenty five years.* (George Beckford lecture series 4) University of the West Indies Press

Lemoine, M. 1985. *Bitter sugar.* London: Zed Press

Levitt, K. 1990. *The origins and consequences of Jamaica's debt crisis 1970-90.* University of the West Indies Press

Levitt, K. 2000. *The George Beckford papers.* Selected and introduced by Kari Levitt (comp) University of West Indies Press, with the George Beckford Foundation

MacDonald, S. and Fauriol, G. 1991. *The politics of the Caribbean basin sugar trade.* New York: Praeger.

Manley, M. 1982. *Jamaica – struggle on the periphery.* London: Third World Media Limited

Manley, M. 1997. *The poverty of nations: reflections on underdevelopment and the world economy.* Pluto Press

McGregor, A. (et al) 1979. *The Barbados sugar industry: problems and perspectives.* Institute of Commonwealth Studies, London

Mills Commission 1988 *Report of the sugar industry enquiry commission (1987/88).* Government offices, Kingston, Jamaica

Mordecai Commission 1967 *Report of the sugar industry enquiry commission (1966).* Government printer, Kingston, Jamaica

Plant, R. 1987. *Sugar and modern slavery – a tale of two countries.* Zed Books

Pollitt, B. and Hagelburg, G. 1994. *The Cuban sugar economy in the Soviet era and after.* Cambridge Journal of Economics, Vol 18, 547-569

Ridgeway, J. (eds) 1994. *The Haiti Files: decoding the crisis.* London: Latin America Bureau

Sanchez, R. 1964. *Sugar and society in the Caribbean.* Yale

Stubbs, J. 1989. *Cuba: the Test of Time.* London: Latin America Bureau

Sugar Industry Research Institute 1992. *Sugar industry perspectives for the year 2000.* Sugar Industry Research Institute, Mandeville, Jamaica

Tate and Lyle 1964. *WISCO in Jamaica: a brief history of sugar in Jamaica and the contribution made by Tate and Lyle.* London

Thomas, C. Y. 1984. *Plantations, peasants and the state: a study of the mode of sugar production in Guyana.* University of the West Indies Press

Watson, J. 1979. *The West Indian heritage: a history of the West Indies.* London: Cox and Wyman Ltd

William, E. 1970. *From Columbus to Castro: the history of the Caribbean, 1492-1969.* André Deutsch, op.cit.

Chapter Six

Christian Aid 1996. *The global supermarket: Britain's biggest shops and food from the Third World.* London: Christian Aid

Ellis, C. 1997. *The urgency for very small states to articulate specific strategies for globalization.* (13th Adlith Brown Memorial Lecture) CCMS/University of the West Indies Press

Jessop, D. and Lowe, M. 1999. *Supporting private sector-led development in the Caribbean – a discussion document on possible avenues for EU support in a successor arrangement to the Lomé Convention.* London: Caribbean Council for Europe

Index